SLEEP
AND LEARN

SLEEP
AND LEARN

by

David Curtis

ROBERT LENI CORP., Publishers
New York

Preface by the Author

Since the appearance of the first edition of *Learn While You Sleep*, I have received letters from a substantial number of people all over the world. This has, of course, been extremely gratifying. I had been a user of the technique for many years, yet I hesitated to attempt to compile the great quantity of facts necessary for a complete evaluation of sleep-learning. However, as I got into the material, I found the information so deeply engrossing, it was soon filling all of my available time.

Through this book I made the acquaintance of many highly interesting and informed people who willingly helped me with this new revised edition.

Mr. Hugo Gernsback's writings on sleep-learning, which go back as far as 1911, were inadvertently left out of the first edition. His original concept of the potential of the technique, advanced thinking even in 1911, is still to be reached today.

I have been in touch with sleep-learning researchers, among them, the Self-Development Research Foundation. They have been of great help in compiling this new edition by allowing me entry to their files.

I have been alternately commended and damned for my work in this field. Personally, I am pleased that the use of the technique is more widespread than it was at my first writing.

My prime concern is that there be understanding of the need for constant learning, awake or asleep. There is, after all, little difference in the basic learning technique. The question of how we learn is under constant appraisal. However, WHY we learn is now very evident. We learn because we want to learn. We learn because there is a reward at the end of the learning path for us.

The business of how is involved with theoretical surmise. And these surmises can change from time to time as newer information on the capacities of man are discovered.

However, we all understand that learning is highly emotional. As such, we can offer ourselves 'goodies' if we will learn. And we find the successful student has learned to motivate himself with rewards of his own choosing.

We also find that learning, awake or asleep, is based on the same concepts. What then is the advantage of sleep-learning?

Let us consider the part repetition plays in learning; we understand that information repeated is more easily learned. Sleep-learning then is actually a time-saver. The material repeated by the automatic repeating cartridge takes over mechanically the repetition process.

Now, concentration. Awake we have the increasingly overpowering diversions of outside noises, problems, dissociation from the material because of lack of interest. In sleep-learning, no diversions are possible. Concentration on the material to be learned then becomes a matter of absolute fact.

Motivation, the next, or, possibly, the most important

consideration in learning, awake or asleep. During sleep-study you listen to material you have recorded yourself. Your need to learn is evidenced by the very fact that you troubled to prepare this material, and you will listen to it with full and complete interest.

No one can explain how all this actually works. I only know that it does, and when you finish this book I trust you will have been stirred to continue further . . . toward learning . . . awake or asleep. Our fate and hope lies in the ability to learn constantly and productively.

Again, I will be pleased to hear from you if you have any new information regarding sleep-learning. However, please do not ask for my recommendation for equipment.

To my wife, Elly, thanks again for your understanding while I was on this project.

David Curtis.

Foreword

"For now we see through a glass, darkly; but then face to face."

Such, I have found, are the processes of general education. Frequently, in my course on World Cultures, I have been able to gain my students' interest by demonstrating the truth of these ancient words quite literally. I ask them to look out the window and watch the cars in the street. Then I tell them to refocus their eyes and look at the glass only, and they invariably notice that it is not very clean. Possibly they were aware as soon as they entered the classroom that the windows needed washing; perhaps all they were conscious of was that the room has windows. In any case many different things present themselves to the eyes and minds of students at the same time, and the good teacher knows how to channel their attention to a few specifics. Once he has done this he must remember the importance of repetition, for in the combination of repetition and attention lies the heart of learning. Further, he knows that repetition by rote is valueless unless the material is accurately absorbed in the beginning. Only correct practice makes perfect.

Whenever I make an assignment I am careful to enter it in my plan book. I have learned from experience that some students will prepare the wrong assignment because they were only half listening, or because they copied it from the board incorrectly. And, of course, they never understand how they happened to make the mistake.

Occasionally I record lectures on tape and play them back. Students tell me that they hear things on the tape that they had not heard during the original lecture. And later on, at quiz time, someone will ask if I ever mentioned a particular point. Once again I expose him to the tape, and he is amazed that he never remembered any reference to the subject before. I explain to him that his mind must have been somewhere else during those words, not because of any deliberate inattention, but for purely unconscious reasons.

A teacher is forever trying out new ways of keeping his students' interest, or of attracting it when it is absent. If only he could hold the attention of every member of the class! Even though they may all be looking directly at the instructor, there are always a few who wander off momentarily, daydreaming without even knowing it. But I have found that this seldom happens when I give private instruction. I have no problem when the student is directly in front of me. The problem appears when he leaves me, for I have no control over his home life, where he may be disturbed by television, radio or countless other annoyances while studying or reviewing his work. No matter how close I came to solving the problem I could never quite put my finger on the best method of improving the process of learning. It was only when I read the galley proofs of *Sleep and Learn* that it became clear to me.

I remembered G.I.'s on a ship in the South Pacific, heading for New Guinea. They played records over and over again in order to learn the native tongue. One evening I was surprised to see friends in the Message Center sleeping with earphones on, and this group learned the language most rapidly, impressing the officer in charge. Others, who spent their evenings smoking, chatting, gambling, or writing letters, said they had no time for extra study, and were told by a member of the advanced group what the secret was.

"The truth is," he explained, "I study during the day just as you do, but each day I learn more than you, because I've broken the barrier—I know the elementary words and phrases—and now it's fun to hear the next lesson. But still, after I've written my letters and relaxed, just before I go to bed, I put the earphones on and listen once more to what I heard during the day. With the earphones on I find I block out all disturbances and discover myself in a new world of learning. When I awake, most of what I heard is part of my new language."

This stayed with me. I thought about the idea often, but I never got around to trying it out or examining its worth. Now this has been done for me, in *Sleep and Learn*.

I recalled another incident out of the past while reading this illuminating book. I was in Gouda, Holland confined for several days in the Diaconnessan de Wyck Hospital, and not allowed to use my eyes. The nurse came over and handed me a little rectangular sponge rubber object, about four or five inches long, to which a cord was attached. She explained that there was a little speaker in the sponge rubber, and if I wished I could put the instrument under my pillow and listen to music for relaxation. The speaker's volume was very low, so low that at first I heard nothing. But when I turned my ear to the pillow I heard everything plainly. Since I was an American, the nurse turned in the BBC for me.

The curtains were drawn all day so that I would not be tempted to use my eyes. When I closed my eyes and listened on the BBC to the news of England, my memories were reawakened. London was mentioned, and I saw myself walking through all the areas I had visited in the cosmopolitan city. With these memories in mind I dozed off. When I awoke I remembered things about London of which I was not conscious before I fell asleep, and I realized that I hadn't dreamed these new memories, even though I saw vivid pictures in my sleep. These were pictures I had previously viewed while walking the streets from Marble Arch to Picadilly Square, only a few weeks earlier. As everyone knows, it is not possible to see everything in London in the course of one walk, but always, with each succeeding walk, I was surprised to note that I had passed various sights the day before without realizing consciously that I had seen them the first time. Now, with the little speaker under my pillow setting the stage for me, I found myself recalling myriad things about London, things which, only a few moments earlier, I did not believe I had seen!

This was a new and startling experience for me. As an educator I wanted to follow through on it, and investigate this process of learning while sleeping. But my time was taken up with many other activities—traveling, setting up new courses in World Cultures, trying to understand students with normal I.Q.'s who repeatedly failed in all subjects but one. I was experimenting in these fields, and was unable to turn my attention to this fascinating business of absorbing knowledge while asleep.

Sleep and Learn reports concisely (but fully) the views of the great scholars of the past and present on this subject. Their conclusions about methods of learning, about memory, and about the role of the unconscious in the process of learning and recall are summarized and considered in relation to this approach which I call "learning plus." The idea of learning in one's sleep is not new. But because our modern world offers so many ingenious devices educators are able, for the first time, to help their students learn more effectively. Valuable time can be saved, freeing the student (and here I use the word student in its broadest sense) for more advanced thought and further study in related fields.

Educators have never found any one method equally effective for all people. Some students never learned to spell until Fernald discovered her unique system. In any subject, some grasp more quickly than others. Similarly, some will learn more rapidly than others when using mechanical sleep-learning devices. But certainly most people should be helped.

If we are to get the most out of life, if we are to make human endeavor meaningful and satisfying, the importance of learning cannot be overemphasized. With the availability of sleep-learning equipment a new world has been opened up to both educators and students. The increased capacity for experiencing and remembering which it offers sparks the imagination and excites greater interest in learning than ever before. I am sure many readers will find the thoughtful and objective evaluation in *Sleep and Learn* both interesting and provocative —as I did.

—Woodman E. Huplits, Jr., D. Ed.

Contents

SLEEP
AND LEARN

chapter I

What Is Sleep-Learning?

Successful learning has always been associated with intensive poring over study material, often far into the night. Hard work through conscious application was the path to successful learning.

Today, with a more complete understanding of our mental abilities, it is possible to be equally conscientious without working nearly so hard. It is, in fact, possible to sleep on the subject—quite literally—and learn it faster and more thoroughly than the most determined application allowed in the past.

This technique of study is called sleep-learning.

Sleep-learning, is based on the known receptivity of the subconscious to suggestion and instruction during the sleeping period.

The principles of sleep-learning were well known to the ancients. In the reign of the Pharaohs, priests recited the scriptures of the period to sleeping novitiates in specially built slumber temples. The priests knew that this would result in a hastening of the learning process,

1

although they didn't understand the mental processes that brought about this accelerated learning. In both Egypt and Greece, the people brought their problems to such temples. There, priests whispered helpful suggestions in their ears. The nocturnal advice dealt primarily with matters of health, general living and the encouragement of confidence.

In informal ways we have been applying the principle of sleep-learning all along. We often decide to "sleep on" a problem we have been unable to solve and then awake with the answer. Many great, inventive personalities have used this approach to highly successful ends; among them, Thomas Alva Edison, who, aided by highly publicized "cat naps" in his laboratory, found a direction to his many discoveries that contributed to our modern way of life.

While we are asleep, some watchful part of us prevents us from rolling out of bed, or pulls the covers up when they have slipped. Mothers, who sleep through traffic noises, thunderstorms and husbands snoring, awake at the slightest sound from their babies. The subconscious functions while we sleep. It has been proven that it can be directed into channels of our choice.

As is the case with so many technological achievements of our time, sleep-learning found its first understanding among the writers of science fact and fiction. The earliest of these, a leader in the understanding of the potential of mankind, and the acknowledged "father" of science fiction, was Hugo Gernsback. He first revealed the modern, mechanical technique with his short story, "Ralph" 124C 41+, published in 1911, in his magazine, *Modern Electrics*. Mr. Gernsback continued with his belief in the technique with an article in *Science and Invention,* December, 1921. After further study and research, in 1923, another article appeared in *Radio News,* in which Chief Radioman J. N. Phinney, U. S. Navy, related his actual work with the technique at the Navy Training School at Pensacola, Florida, in 1922. Here the students were successfully taught Morse code while they slept.

Mr. Gernsback's work in the technique has been discussed in national periodicals since 1944, among them *Time, Coronet,* and *Magazine Digest.*

As with much of the vision shown in Mr. Gernsback's writings, his conception of the technique extends even beyond today's capacities. However, since so many of his "fiction" materials have become fact, we can only hope that his perceptive writings will continue.

Other writers have considered the technique of sleep-learning as a "control" over the mind. In 1932, Aldous Huxley envisioned a new world in which sleep-teaching would be used for purposes of conditioning future citizens along lines considered useful for the state, rather than for intellectual improvement. The methods Huxley described are almost identical with those now in use. He speaks of a continuous, repetitious whisper under the pillow. The degree of his prophetic talent is apparent to people familiar with modern sleep-teaching equipment in which a pillow speaker is attached to a clock-controlled tape recorder. The speaker's volume is just loud enough to reach only the ear of the sleep-learner and the material is repeated several times during the night.

More than a quarter of a century later, in *Brave New*

World Revisited, Huxley discussed the facts then known about sleep-learning. He was concerned about the possibility of misuse, but at the same time recognized that factual material was being successfully taught to sleeping people. Understanding the principles of self-determination and suggestion have shown us that no suggestion, however powerful, may be accepted without the complete acquiescence of the learner.

Responsible proponents of sleep-learning point out that the possibility of misuse exists in most scientific fields, but since the control is individual, we may expect a responsible person to accept only beneficial suggestions.

Continuing research is more firmly establishing that one can learn while asleep. Notable among studies whose findings have led to world-wide experimentation are the work at the University of North Carolina, The University of California, William and Mary Parsons Training School, U.C.L.A., Georgetown University and the Institute of Logopedics. Successful work is being done with the children at the Northside Clinic in New York City and in Bergamo, Italy.

There is considerable interest in some medical circles about the pain-reducing or pain-eliminating faculties of sleep-suggestion.

It is known that childbirth has been rendered painless with the aid of this technique. Indeed, in 1951, the Soviet Union passed a law making it compulsory for doctors to consider this method for every mother-to-be. Although many doctors still question sleep-learning, there are a growing number who, after investigation, are beginning to apply its principles.

Psychiatrists have evinced particular interest in the

potential value of sleep-learning in therapy. A May 1960 article in a leading New York newspaper reported on a paper presented to the scientific session of the American Psychiatric Association in Atlantic City by Dr. M. Ralph Kaufman, of the Mount Sinai Hospital, which stated:

> The situation is such that psychoanalysis that began as hypnotherapy . . . has now given us the kind of understanding of hypnotic suggestion which makes it available as a therapeutic measure for psychotherapy.

An increasing number of college students supplement their daytime work with sleep-study. Testimonials from both instructors and students in learning institutions indicate better results in examinations resulting from their use of sleep-learning techniques. Language instructors as well as their students report that the method of study speeds up the learning process considerably.

A mid-western lecturer states that his memorization rate increased by 75%.

A blind student finds the technique uniquely helpful and practical.

Parents write that young children, whose studies involve a great deal of rote-learning, benefit considerably.

Divinity students foresee greater information accumulation potential through the use of the technique of sleep-education.

A college instructor prepares his lecture material with sleep-learning.

The memory-training qualities of this technique seem to be of particular value to people who must remember specialized data. Television presented to the American public a young man who learned conversational French while asleep, under controlled test conditions. After only one week of sleep-learning, he was examined by Dr. Adrian Miller, professor of Romance Languages at U.C.L.A., on the television program, "You Asked For It." The Professor's judgement was that the young man had absorbed the equivalent of a SEMESTER of class-room study.

Others report considerable help in the learning or appreciation of music. Television actors, among them Larry Blyden and Marilyn Erskine, have learned complete roles quickly with the aid of sleep-learning equipment. Metropolitan Opera star Ramon Vinay not only quickly memorized a leading operatic role but also learned to sing it in perfect, accentless Italian. Equally successful results have been reported by people of various language backgrounds in learning English, free of foreign accent.

At the Institute of Logopedics, in Wichita, Kansas, where experiments were conducted to find out whether nocturnal education could help cure speech defects, the results showed that students who heard a list of words while they were sleeping memorized and improved much faster than the control group which did not apply sleep-learning.

At the Northside Clinic in New York City, a young boy of sixteen whose basic problem was retention of study material, significantly increased his retentive powers.

Numerous famous personalities have attested to the benefits of sleep-study. Alexander de Seversky eliminated his Russian accent. Rudy Vallee, Bing Crosby and Gloria Swanson have learned lines and lyrics this way.

Perhaps the most impressive example of the retentive powers of the subconscious during sleep is that of Art Linkletter, radio and television star. In full view of the millions who watch his program, Linkletter offered to test the theory by attempting to sleep-learn the most difficult language in the world—Mandarin Chinese. After sleep-studying for only ten nights, Linkletter invited the Vice Consul of China to his TV show, introduced him in a pleasant conversation in Mandarin Chinese. The Vice-Consul's verdict was that Linkletter was indeed conversant in the language and would be able to travel throughout China and be understood perfectly by anyone who speaks the Mandarin dialect.

It is, however, highly questionable that everyone should expect such spectacular results. In all study techniques, it is accepted that we will learn material we have some familiarity with easier and faster. In subsequent contact with Mr. Linkletter, it seems that he is not anxious to pursue his extravagant claims further.

It is now known that during World War II, members of the armed forces of the United States were taught the Morse code and foreign languages, in a necessarily brief period, with the aid of sleep-learning. The renowned Office of Strategic Services (O.S.S.) taught its agents not only languages but also slang, accents and customs of the countries to be infiltrated. They learned quickly and thoroughly.

An oil company in Arabia employs sleep-learning for

teaching English to its native employees and Arabic to its American staff.

In 1955, Canada's Department of National Defense used sleep-learning in the training of Royal Air Force personnel. These men scored consistently higher than a control group of non-users.

Business has also been quick to recognize how sleep-study can help build up sales. *The Wall Street Journal* of March 14, 1958, reported on a group of corporations using sleep-learning to develop self-confidence and sales ability and techniques to bolster the effectiveness of their salesmen.

Minnesota Mining and Manufacturing Company, an industrial and marketing giant, has had its salesmen use the technique of sleep-study to assimilate information about their products and the sales techniques preferred by the company to sell these products.

This approach has also proved invaluable to many who must remember special technical facts or figures. A railroad dispatcher memorized the entire passenger train schedule of the Union Pacific Railroad in 10 days. A post office employee memorized commercials accurately and quickly and remembered them at will while on the air. A production executive in a large advertising firm memorized nearly 600 telephone numbers of frequent usage.

Unusual and successful experiments in sleep-teaching are reported by a professor who taught Greek to his five-year-old child by whispering in his ear as he slept; by a pastor whose eleven-year-old son memorized four pages of poetry overnight (while the rest of his class

8

learned two pages a week); by a man who taught his parakeet 1,300 words; by a 63-year-old grandmother who is memorizing the New Testament; by a writer who is memorizing the dictionary at the rate of three pages a night.

Psychotherapists submit favorable reports on the use of sleep-teaching techniques for implanting therapeutic suggestions in the subconscious mind to supplement treatment during waking hours.

"There appears to be enough evidence to indicate that treatment during sleep is not only possible in theory but also in practice," writes Dr. Ernst Schmidhofer, chief of the Neuropsychiatric Service of the Memphis Veterans Administration Hospital.

Psychologists have also reported success in breaking bad habits ranging from overeating to speech defects. Mothers, following their suggestions, have been able to train their children out of thumb sucking, bed wetting and nail biting through the use of sleep-education.

A great many diseases and mental disorders are psychosomatic symptoms of a subconscious block; it is felt that the inner conflict must be recognized and faced consciously by the patient if he hopes to overcome the problem. Since suggestion is a tool of psychotherapy, it must be concluded that self-recorded therapeutic messages (sleep-tapes) can take their rightful place beside drugs and hypnosis as an effective means for reaching the subconscious.

Certainly the cases reported indicate that there is a great value potential in this form of therapy. It has been stated that sleep-suggestion may eventually replace medical hypnosis, since doctors and psychiatrists not sufficiently schooled in the technique of hypnosis, can easily prepare a sleep-tape.

It has been firmly established throughout recent years that repetitive suggestion is the most direct route to successful learning. The basic technique of sleep-learning has placed a pattern of operation on this method.

We shall see what this means to the sincere student who is anxious to develop both emotionally and educationally.

chapter II

The Logic of Sleep Learning

Why is the conscious mind unable to absorb facts as quickly as the subconscious? Samuel Taylor Coleridge, related the case of the twenty-five-year-old woman who could not read or write, but who, during a seizure of what was then known as brain fever, spoke Latin, Greek and Hebrew incessantly and in very pompous tones. It was known that she had been a servant to a Protestant pastor for many years. She had subconsciously absorbed the passages he read aloud to himself as he walked up and down a hallway adjoining the kitchen. Notes taken during her delirium coincided with passages in books which the pastor owned.

The theory, most often stated by the authorities in the field of sleep-education, is that the subconscious is not hampered by the daily needs for diversified thinking that the conscious mind requires. It is a simple fact that we, in our daily lives, are faced with myriad distractions which tend to keep us from direct concentration. However, during sleep, we are at our most relaxed, and our subconscious mind is open to receive the material we want to learn—without interference.

It has been firmly established that most thinking and sorting of facts is done subconsciously; our conscious minds are aware only of the results of this thinking.

When we give up trying to remember a particular piece of information which we have filed in our mind, we find that the answer to our problem arrives without any concentrated effort on our part. Obviously, the information we accumulate is stored in our minds, and given the natural opportunity, will make itself available as we require it.

Repetition of acts, which are learned consciously, although executed very slowly at first (walking for instance), makes these acts easier to perform, until finally the effort involved becomes less than the minimum necessary for consciousness. The rapidity and dexterity with which we perform many actions, make us unconscious of these actions. This same ease and speed, the proponents of sleep-learning feel, are attainable in a great many areas of mental training. This feeling seems to be well substantiated in fact.

Much of our knowledge lies beneath the surface of our consciousness, ready to be recalled when the need arises. It would be impossible for us to function if every bit of information in the mind were always present in our awareness. Selectivity and concentration would be seriously hampered by the distraction of too many ideas, for our brains record every impression, every thought we ever had, every action we have ever performed. And, there seems to be no limit to the capacity of the brain to collect, store, and make available any and all types of information. This record is obviously permanent, and effects all of our actions and feelings throughout our lives. It remains in the subconscious, ready to be associated with a conscious idea or need, in a process of which we are completely unaware. Consciously we may forget a great deal, but all the memories, all the ideational and imaginative capacities, are there in our subconscious. They flash into our conscious minds suddenly and without effort, or, we are able to remember them consciously by association.

This subconscious selectivity of material for our conscious minds is the key to concentration of attention during which we absorb consciously that which we have focused on, but exclude all other impressions of our senses. We exclude them, that is, from our consciousness, but the subconscious will notice and absorb them. The subconscious is able to supply the information when it is needed, if the necessary conditions of relaxation and receptivity are present.

Relaxation and receptivity to suggestion are the principles behind sleep-learning. They make it possible for students to perform feats impossible for them during conditions of consciousness. The retentive power of the subconscious acounts for people carrying out post-hypnotic suggestions. It is these same principles of relaxation and receptivity to suggestion (suggestion concentrates the attention of the subconscious), on which sleep-learning is based.

The reticular theory of consciousness, a new explanation of how the brain works, puts forth the hypothesis that the nerve cells performing the highest level of integration are deep within the brain, not in the outer layer or cortex. This inner system is known as the reticular system, and the theory is that the cortex gives meaning to the incoming stimuli and stores these meanings for future reference. The cortex also condenses, edits and transmits the sense stimuli to the reticular system for final integration into meaning. Then the reticular system sends out impulses to sensory motor regions of the cortex which will induce a muscular response.

According to this theory, it is not only the cortex, but also the midbrain (subconscious) which can store patterns of learned behavior. The cortex plays an important role in the learning of motor activity, but in time this is bypassed and the reticular system and the subcortical motor centers take over most of the work. The electroencephalograph, a machine which records brain activity, has shown us that the subconscious is receptive and alert twenty-four hours a day, and has established proof that the subconscious mind can absorb for that full period.

Proceeding from this knowledge, sleep-learning authorities base their approach on the established fact that the subconscious receives and retains all stimuli regardless of whether the subject is awake or asleep. Similarities have been noted between some stages of hypnosis and normal sleep, in that the same influences can bring about either state. Elimination of strong stimuli, a position of rest, gentle, monotonous stimulation of the sense organs, dismissal of disturbing thoughts—all these, added to the students passivity, have been accepted as proven methods for putting people to sleep, either naturally or hypnotically. The influence of suggestion has operated not only on people in a hypnotic state, but on people in light sleep as well. In dreams, we accept without question many things which our conscious minds would reject, as do people under hypnosis.

Most people are susceptible to suggestion during their waking hours. Indeed, it is difficult to find someone who has not responded to suggestion. In every life situation, we are exposed to many subtle suggestions, all of which influence us. We catch moods; we yawn involuntarily when we see another yawn; we pick up rhythms; we respond to ideas under the influence of charm and affection. We accept much on faith in fields other than our own; we are influenced by books, clothing, atmosphere, words. We are educated by suggestion, to a great extent, and receive moral and religious instruction in the same way. In time we develop a large reservoir of autosuggestions.

It is because of our suggestibility that we respond to the arts, that we buy what we buy, responding to the advertiser's repetitions. Suggestibility in the voter becomes evident at the polls. Broad social movements and mob action could never occur if it were not for the fact that humans are highly suggestible.

It is in a relaxed state—or in any other state where the reasoning function is less active that we are most amenable to suggestion, and this fact appears to be responsible for the efficiency in learning that is claimed by adherents of the sleep-study school. Relaxation increases with sleep, and so the subconscious is even more easily reached by suggestion than it is during waking hours, and is taught more effectively.

Sleep-learning, since it is predicated on suggestion and repetition, avoids the necessity of waiting for the conscious mind to open the door for the desired information. It slips in more easily, unhindered, because the door to the subconscious is always open.

During sleep, during periods of relaxation, mental stress is at a minimum. Since learning is most easily absorbed under favorable emotional conditions, and since the mind is so receptive to suggestions under these conditions sleep-learning reflects the benefits of many advantages not always possible during waking hours. It is no longer necessary to make a conscious effort to concentrate, to eliminate distracting thoughts, or to call up the will to learn. The procedure, as described, is to begin to listen to the recorded message until you fall asleep, then continue for approximately two hours during the early sleep-period. It is also advised that reinforcement be obtained for the period starting approximately one and one half-hours before awakening.

There has been much talk of the "barrier." This term is used to describe the would-be student who finds that he is not receiving the recorded material. In most studied cases, it has become evident that the "barrier," is rightly to be termed "self-induced barrier" since this is precisely the problem; the student has developed, through his own anxiety, a block against the acceptance of the recorded material. The answer to this seems to be relaxation. We are all aware that the learning processes are more easily activated during periods of relaxation. Simply put, the capacity to learn seems to be a basic instinct, and the only obstruction to this is self-induced. The psychological block against learning while asleep then, is most easily overcome through relaxation. In a great many instances, recording relaxation affirmations that will repeat during the sleep-study periods will overcome this "barrier."

The importance of relaxation affirmations for the difficult sleep-student is stressed because of the tensions and frustrations that are a part of our life, and which can be at work, even during sleep. It is universally suggested that a few recommendations be in constant consideration when using the technique of sleep-learning:

Short messages at the beginning; using a poem for the first learning attempt, since the alliteration and rhythm is conducive to early acceptance of the recorded material.

Consistency of sleep-study—without even a single night's interruption if possible.

Conscientiousness and genuine desire to succeed.

Avoidance of alcohol, drugs, barbiturates, or tranquilizers, which induce a heavy, unnatural sleep.

Confidence and overcoming of anxiety.

Delay of study, instead using sleep-therapy affirmations during illness and recuperation.

Specialists in sleep-learning are unable to state with certainty how long it will take to absorb a message in sleep-study. They do know that for most people the number of impressions (repetitions) necessary to memorize material during sleep is most certainly a great deal less than the number needed while awake.

The experiments of Dr. Wilder Penfield of the Montreal Neurological Institute established that the natural tape recorders in our heads require only one impression for retention—possibly lifelong. Dr. Denfield discovered this during surgery on patients under local anaesthesia. He stimulated certain brain cells with gentle electric current and the patients, who were conscious, reported perfect playbacks of conversations, songs, and other experiences as far back as childhood.

Despite the knowledge that one impression is sufficient to register permanently on our brain, repetition appears to be necessary to memorize material. The reason for this is not yet known. It is thought that there may be some relationship between the time the impression is made and the ability to recall it when awake. Sleep-learning psychologists hope to discover a means of triggering off recall much as the electric current did in Dr. Penfield's experiments. Meanwhile, sleep-memorization is based on repetition and free-association.

Certain things have been found to be helpful in aiding retention of material. Motivation is important, as, for instance, thinking of the reward that will be enjoyed as a result of learning a particular material. Material that is understood is retained better than material learned by rote alone; repetition alone will affect memorization, but intelligent memorization will lead to the proper, profitable use of the material learned. Writing the material after sleep-learning has helped toward permanent memorization, and repetition a few times after the material is learned aids in retention. New forms of presentation are no more effective than repetition of identical material; the latter is recommended to refresh the memory.

The order of presentation seems to be important: the beginning and end of a lengthy sleep-study period are often remembered better than the middle parts, which seems to emphasize that the sleep-student should not attempt too much material in one night's sleep-study.

The maximum to date of material that will be accepted in its entirety seems to be just under one-half hour in length. There is, by the way, a great deal of information that may be learned in a half-hour.

In learning a language it appears more effective to place the English translation ahead of the foreign language. A therapist in New York, studying Russian, found that after using sleep-learning her studies during conscious, waking periods, gave her the feeling that she was indeed, relearning a language she had been familiar with.

New, challenging, interesting material is easier to retain than dull, static, or uninteresting data. Frequently something that seems unavailable for recall (like every one of 1000 new words) will be recognized and understood when the student is confronted with the necessity for recognition.

It is not advisable to try to learn two unrelated subjects in one night; the second subject can diminish or cancel out the first in what sleep-learning psychologists call retroactive inhibition. *It is always important to remember that good results in sleep-learning lead to better results in sleep-learning.*

There is a great deal of evidence of the progressive advantages of using the technique. In the past years, there has been, due to the more conscious understanding of the potential of the human mind, a greater acceptance of the technique, and due to the greater numbers of people using the method, a more substantial case history file has been compiled.

A California pediatrician reports success in as high as 70% of cases in the last twelve years where he has had parents talk to children with bed-wetting problems while they were asleep—and this after only two or three nights' repetition. Today's electronic equipment, of course, save the lung power, in addition to achieving highly effective results.

Therapy combined with sleep has been reported effective in connection with special problems and social betterment. Dr. James Odell, Coordinator of Adjunctive Therapies at the Parsons, Kansas Training School, conducted an experiment with retarded and mentally disturbed children. He selected two young girls with an I.Q. of twenty-five and forty respectively, who had difficulty in pronouncing the letter R! He played a sleep-tape for them on which were various words containing the letter R. This, combined with speech therapy sessions, resulted in the children using the letter R correctly after twenty-one days.

Adults whose problems have landed them in prison have voluntarily participated in a sleep-therapy experiment in the Woodland Road Camp near Visalia, California, in Tulare County. The tape message is based on the belief that a desire for self-punishment is the main reason for crime, and is intended to overcome this desire.

A recording played at specific intervals during the night drones, "Sleep, sleep, you are now completely in sleep. Listen, my inner self. Remember and obey this creed of life. Live. Relax. Completely and utterly relax. Heal my soul. Unite my subconscious with my conscious life. Life is worth living, worth living whole-heartedly. Love rule my life. Love God, family, others. Do to others what I want them to do to me. . . ."

20

Another report of this experiment substitutes "you" for the first person, and continues, "You shall have a major goal in life. You shall plan, carry out and attain that goal. You shall work and share with others. You shall grow in mind and spirit. You will attain self-respect and maturity because you are good . . . you will live without alcohol. You can abstain from alcohol. Alcohol is repulsive to you. . . ."

John Locke, public defender of Tulare, strongly feels that there has been about 50% effectiveness so far, but adds that the test should continue for four or five years before fully assessing results. Some of the prisoners reported benefits. One said he always dreamed of liquor, but after sleep-therapy liquor made him sick to his stomach. Another announced a new belief that people were not "down on him." A third said he could now go to sleep with a clear mind. The Tulare County Board of Supervisors has made "Operation Sleep" a permanent fixture.

Aldous Huxley objects, not to the principle of filling people with love and compassion, but to the principle of sleep-teaching by government agencies. He questions whether the treatment would always be on a voluntary basis, and whether the intentions would always be as good as they are in Tulare County. Mr. Huxley willingly attests to having seen some remarkable results, but remains concerned about would-be mind manipulators. Present research seems to dispel the need for this concern. It has been found that the sleep-student will not allow himself to accept material he does not want to learn.

Undoubtedly caution should be exercised. The Federal Trade Commission is keeping close watch. However, most sleep-learning proponents are sincere in their claims, with honest stipulations as to the actual benefits of sleep-study. There have been very few extravagant claims for the technique. In most instances, full explanation leading to logical conclusions have been the procedure of the reputable sleep-learning organizations. Certainly, it is to be understood that the ability to learn, either consciously or through sleep-learning, varies from person to person.

Age is no barrier to sleep-learning; if the student is conscientious in application, and in reasonably good health (in order that the mental block of bad health should not interfere with the process of learning). There have been many tests that determine positively that people of any age can learn by this method.

It should also be logically assumed that using sleep-therapy for the removal of pain should not be attempted without the advice of a competent medical authority.

The practice of sleep-study has not, as far as is known, produced any harmful effects and, when proper instruction procedures are followed, it is extremely unlikely that any but established results be achieved.

This method is used widely in secondary schools in Soviet Russia, as well as in the treatment of the mentally ill, and even more extensively in other fields of medicine. There, the treatment is based on Pavlov's discoveries. Most certainly the progress of sleep-learning in the U.S.S.R. can be matched anywhere because everyone possesses an infinite capacity to learn; this, combined with sleep-learning will produce highly advantageous results. It must be remembered that we must take advan-

22

tage of our inherent capacities, or, as is evident in many cases, people with high I.Q.'s stagnate through inactivity.

In this country, interest has been rapidly expanding, as are sales among the organizations who offer sleep-study equipment. It is safe to assume it will continue to grow. Even the past few years have shown an amazing increase in the users of the technique. The technique has progressed because of the advances conceived by the electronics industry which has developed the necessary electronic and mechanical components that make sleep-education effective and effortless today.

Certainly, the science of making useful the third of our lives normally spent in sleep is worth complete investigation.

chapter III

The Subconscious

Since sleep-learning is based largely on the capacity of the subconscious to absorb and retain information, let us investigate the knowledge and theories existing about this less familiar area of the brain.

It should be noted that the term subconscious is used in sleep-learning and in literature about hypnosis, but the term is not recognized in psychoanalysis, where it is designated the unconscious. When referred to in sleep-learning, however, it is the subconscious. Remember, there is no area of difference between the terms.

In Freud's imagery, the unconscious was a kind of anteroom to the conscious mind from which excitations are frequently barred by a censorous doorman. This censor is referred to as repression. But, sometimes, these excitations from the unconscious pass the censor without becoming conscious. That is, they are held back by further resistance. This, Freud referred to as the preconscious system. These unconscious processes can be quite powerful and can produce effects and ideas without the conscious mind being aware of the processes involved.

"Unconsciousness," wrote Freud, "is a regular and inevitable phase in the process constituting our mental activity; every mental act begins as an unconscious one, and it may remain so or go on developing into consciousness, according to whether it meets resistance or not."

We are all familiar with the overnight solving of a problem unresolved before sleeping. This is consistent with Freud's comments on nocturnal mental activity in his study of dream processes. He tells us that "unsolved problems, harassing cares, and overwhelming impressions continue the activity of our thoughts even during sleep, maintaining psychic processes in the system which we have termed the preconscious.

"The thought-impulses continued into sleep may be divided into the following groups:

1. Those which have been left uncompleted because our mental powers have failed us, i.e., unsolved problems.

2. Those which have been suppressed and turned back during the day.

3. Those which have been excited in our Ucs. (unconscious).

4. Those which have not been completed during the day owing to some accidental cause.

5. The indifferent impressions of the day, which have therefore been left unsettled."

Freud goes on to point out that the preconscious activity will not become conscious mental processes during sleep. If this were to happen, then we would simply not be asleep.

While discussing unconscious activity in terms of the dream-process, Freud makes an interesting observation which may explain some aspects of the capacity to learn during sleep. He points out that dreams substitute for many daytime thoughts and once investigated and understood, fit together with logic—indicating that the thoughts originate in normal mental life and that the complicated processes of conscious thinking are repeated in dream thoughts. He saw a continuous process from the first stimulus (often not consciously noted, but occurring during waking hours) to its completion at the onset of sleep.

Freud considered this proof that extremely complex mental operations were possible without the cooperation of consciousness.

Freud later made clear that the unconscious, preconscious, and conscious thought development was not a matter of psychic topography. Eventually he concluded that the essential character of a preconscious idea was its connection with the residue of verbal ideas. He asserted that consciousness was overestimated by the psychologists of his day, describing the unconscious as the larger circle which included the smaller circle of the conscious.

Further he wrote that everything conscious has a preliminary unconscious stage, although the reverse is not true. The unconscious, he said, is the "true psychic reality; in its inner nature it is just as much unknown to us as the reality of the external world, and it is just as imperfectly communicated to us by the data of consciousness as is the external world by the reports of our sense organs."

Intellectual achievement during sleep (completion of daytime mental work) is part of the same psychic forces operating intellectually during waking hours. Unconscious activity is related to the "inspiration" experienced by creative thinkers. There is in these moments a concerted effort of the unconscious becoming aware and joining with conscious activity.

Freud developed his concept of the unconscious, preconscious and conscious into the theory of a personality organization of the id, the ego and the super-ego. He did not consider the ego synonymous with consciousness, nor could he specifically separate the preconscious and the unconscious completely, for they revealed certain characteristics in common. The general qualities of the original distinctions were retained, with the id representing the entirely unconscious aspect of mental activity, without organization or will or awareness of the passage of time; the ego is part of the id and is its agent, more affected by the external world, and the seat of intelligence and reason; and separating itself from the ego, in a self-observing and self-critical function, representing the demands of the external world, is the super-ego.

Jung believed that a knowledge greater than man's own lies in the depths of the unconscious. He felt that this knowledge is a collective psyche of the ages as well as the forgotten or unrecognized aspects of individual experience. He taught that the greater the harmony and coordination of the conscious and unconscious, the healthier the individual will be. He spoke of joint activity between the two. He also described the unconscious as continually active. The individual's direction is indicated by the combination of materials in the unconscious —infinitely superior to those in the conscious mind—and thus an "unparalleled guide" for mankind.

Jung based his ideas of the collective unconscious on the fact that motifs of myths and legends are repeated in identical forms all over the world. He recognized two layers in the unconscious, one personal and one transpersonal, the latter common in humanity. The personal memory-images are filled out, because they have been experienced by the individual, but the collective layer, being pre-infantile—residues of ancestral life—and not personally experienced are therefore not filled out.

Jung felt that the unconscious was continually occupied in grouping and regrouping its contents, and normally, this activity is coordinated with the conscious mind in a compensatory relationship.

In discussing susceptibility and mental contagion, Jung spoke of man as having a great capacity for imitation. He noted that this is a doube-edged capacity—valuable for collective purposes but dangerous from the point of view of developing the individual. Development of the individual involves the compensatory relationship between the conscious and the unconscious, which leads to a widened consciousness and a freer participation in the world.

Dollard and Miller believe that reinforcements of all kinds automatically strengthen responses that immediately precede them. They feel that the primary effect of a reinforcement is always unconscious—but that this unconscious reinforcement is mediated by verbal and other cue-producing responses. Overlearning can render responses unconscious and, as a result, verbalization can be short-circuited. Thus automatic (unconscious) habits are formed. But because there was verbalization originally, it is fairly easy to recover the habits from the unconscious after overlearning. A strong drive will intensify the habitual response.

Dr. Bernard Hollander, a lifelong student and practitioner of hypnosis, writes that some psychologists do not accept the existence of the subconscious but, he points out, regardless of terminology or the degree of unconscious or subconscious activity, there obviously exists a large collection of experiences, thoughts and emotions not present in our consciousness at any given moment. He uses the term subconscious as a working hypothesis to explain the source of genius' ideas, inspiration and creativity.

We are conscious only of the result of subconscious thinking, which he says, constitutes much of our thinking. The activity itself remains hidden from us. Many learned acts, by virtue of repetition, become subconscious. Selection of one out of many ideas stimulated by association is a decisive activity of the subconscious. Associative sensory impressions, as we concentrate on a particular subject, are noted by the subconscious, even though we are not consciously aware of them.

Of course, subconscious work is not tiring, as is conscious effort.

Writing of the conscious use of the subconscious mind, Robert D. Updegraff notes that we drive ourselves consciously but use only half our minds. By not relaxing, we keep the subconscious from working for us. He points out, as does Dr. Hollander, that a majority of brilliant men reported that their best discoveries occurred to them when they were _not_ working. Von Helmholtz never got his ideas when he was fatigued or at his work table. Thornton Wilder's inspirations came in the shower or on hikes or in other informal places. Descartes' discoveries came to him in bed in the morning.

Updegraff writes that we can consciously use the subconscious mind, first by organizing the material consciously, then by giving a definite assignment to the subconscious and forgetting it. The material can be written out, or simply discussed with associates, or worked on consciously until exhaustion sets in—and then put aside completely in favor of a relaxing activity or sleep. The subconscious mind will probably finish the job.

Sometimes further conscious work is necessary, but usually the subconscious can be trusted and often does the work more quickly than the conscious mind. Further, says Updegraff, the results are probably better by virtue of the fact that a whole life's experience is brought to bear on the problem.

An interesting footnote to habit-breaking comes from Knight Dunlap. He recommends practicing the bad habit; making the unconscious habit conscious by doing it intentionally, but denouncing the habit while practicing it and also in endeavoring sincerely to break it. This negative practice, was tested and found successful. Dunlap, himself, tried it. He had a habit typing _hte_ instead of _the_ and practiced by typing _hte_ hundreds of times, telling himself each time that he was wrong. The original error was unconscious; he broke the habit by making himself conscious of it.

Since the subconscious is the storehouse of memory and habit, we can fill it during sleep with suggestions of our choice, which we retain better than conscious ideas because then interferences are absent. We know our conscious will accept whatever our subconscious accepts.

Since there is still much to be learned about the subconscious-unconscious, it is impossible to evaluate with certainty all sleep-learning claims. Among authorities however, there is a high degree of acceptancy.

All the authorities whom we have discussed rated unconscious activity as much greater than the conscious. They believe that the unconscious never sleeps. Freud saw dreams as logical processes developed from conscious thought. Jung believed that the unconscious was constantly grouping and regrouping its material, and that harmony and coordination between the unconscious and conscious could be achieved to a greater degree, with infinitely more satisfactory results to the individual. In sleep-learning, too, the assumption is made that the subconscious has a capacity for assorting, selecting and arranging material and that the danger of universal conformity can be allayed by conscious interpretation of the unconsciously learned material.

Dollard and Miller's discussion of overlearning can be directly related to sleep-learning. Reinforcement is an important part of sleep-learning and daytime recall can perhaps be explained in terms of cue-producing responses. Sleep-learning is verbal and should be considered as an important new aspect of the thought process.

Dr. Hollander's description of subconscious activity comes closest to explaining the process by which we learn in our sleep. Ideas are suggested to the subconscious, which absorbs them and supplies them to the conscious when they are needed, by its own mysterious process of selection. Repetition renders many learned acts unconscious and these are always accessible to us—barring repressive disturbances.

Updegraff attests that the subconscious can be put to use consciously and deliberately. Sleep-learners simply go one step further.

Sleep-learners' experience in breaking habits indicates that Dunlap's time-effort-consuming approach to negative practice is unnecessary self-punishment.

The power of the subconscious can apparently be harnessed through sleep-learning.

chapter IV

Theories of Learning

How do we learn?

Theories have been expounded through the ages in attempts to explain the process of acquiring knowledge. The ancients formed theories consistent with their philosophies and in terms of their particular culture. More recent thinkers tried to veer away from the completely abstract interpretations in favor of answers which could be better related to tangible evidence. Modern psychologists have been concerned with establishing a physiological basis for their theories. They are circumspect in conducting careful experiments and tabulating results with mathematical exactitude, determined to meet the requirements of a scientific age. Others, particularly in the field of education, indicate that they find the human element somewhat elusive in their laboratory and add to their interpretations consideration of social environment and personality factors.

Since people who promulgate theories have a noticeable tendency to gather evidence supporting their par-

33

ticular beliefs, there is a strong case made for nearly every school of thought. However, there is an undeniable degree of similarity among the varied points of view.

The basic fact they have in common is the simple truth that man does learn. He learns from the moment he is born. He learns through direct and indirect means, through informal and formal instruction. Sometimes he learns in spite of instruction. Sometimes he applies himself assiduously with discouraging results and other times he suddenly knows with little or no apparent effort. Sometimes he learns to be socially useful; sometimes he acquires skills which are adjudged harmful and negative. But he learns.

Non-human animals learn too, and rats and dogs have contributed greatly to the formation of theories of learning. Machines have been devised to take over many of our thinking processes but the business of learning goes on in one form or another, in the course of growing and participating in life.

But, how do we learn?

True to his principles, Socrates thought of learning and of knowledge as part of universal and eternal verities. For him, man was simply an example of the truth of eternal knowledge. But the mechanism behind man's personal awareness of this knowledge was something that Socrates did not attempt to explain.

For Plato the idea was supreme; only reason counted for anything. As for experience, it was merely a shadow of the idea of reality. Sensations and opinions, he held, are passing and unreliable. The immaterial essences— Forms or Ideas—were absolute for him, containing the only ultimate truth.

While the Greeks are philosophically stimulating, they fail to answer our question. However, we must consider the culture which produced such theories. Here was a society in which the individual counted for little, in which slaves were bought and sold, in which human life was cheaply held. As a result, a philosophy developed which expressed the need for security and permanence. Almost inevitably, on the basis of this explanation, abstract ideals of truth which exist above and beyond the individual were developed as absolutes.

Consider the mania for efficiency and speed in all areas of contemporary life. Is it surprising that the same influences are felt in the fields of learning and self-development? Consider the ever-increasing swarm of push-buttons which almost seem to run our lives. There are so many areas in which physical effort has been reduced to a minimum that perhaps we are ready to eliminate mental effort as well. The easy way is always the tempting way and, if the results are even better, why not take advantage of a time and labor-saving device?

In the area of psychotherapy we find there is a widespread need for professional help and, once again, we observe the temptation to do it the modern, easy way, to save time and money and effort. There is certainly a special appeal to those people who feel that they don't need extensive professional guidance, since they have only a few minor difficulties to work out. Whether or not this self-evaluation is correct, sleep-learning offers man an opportunity to take the easy way out.

Finally, in this age when education is nearly universal, the amassing of facts is considered an important achievement and, in the cases of the now-defunct quiz shows, a lucrative one. We are supposed to know something about everything—and there is so much to know. There just isn't enough time during waking hours. Often we are too tired to even care about improving ourselves.

Yes, sleep-learning has much modern appeal.

Still, only by knowing how we learn can we examine the effectiveness of sleep-learning. There is not, of course, complete agreement among authorities but if we can unearth points on which they do agree then we can evaluate sleep-learning against accepted theories.

Looking back a few centuries (1690), we find John Locke challenging the old doctrine that men come into the world with a set of ideas and a particular character stamped on their minds. He argued that knowledge was derived from experience, the result of ideas acquired through the five senses, and from inner experiences of the mind which operate in considering the ideas derived from sensations.

Only what can be perceived exists, according to George Berkeley (1710), and various combinations of perceptions come to signify objects or ideas. The perceiving is done by a distinct entity, the self, and nothing can exist except in the mind which perceives it. Berkeley asserted that all reality was mental and all nature a manifestation of God.

David Hume later (1748) affirmed that there was no knowledge beyond the evidence of the senses, that there was no such thing as cause and effect and that experience was primary in all thinking. He divided the mind's perceptions into impressions (sensations, passions, emotions) and ideas by which he meant the faint images of impressions in thinking and reasoning.

A pioneer in psychological research, Johann Friedrich Herbart (1816) held that the mind is a blank on which experience writes, man learns by means of perception of the sense organs and by the process of association. Herbart attempted to explain psychic phenomena in terms of simple ideas and looked forward to a future system of psychodynamics determined by mathematical laws.

Wilhelm Wundt, who founded the first psychological laboratory (1879) denied rationalism. He devised experimental methods for measuring reactions to physical and physiological changes, effects and stimulations. But he did not consider the physiological aspect to be all of psychology. He was concerned with introspection, with analysis of "internal experience." He was convinced that the combination of the will, and emotional states closely connected with it, was more important than sensations and ideas in the explanation of psychological experience.

Another physiological-psychological approach was presented by Herbert Spencer (1855), who saw man as an organism adapting to its environment. He felt that sensations are man's natural guides and his most trustworthy ones—"when not rendered morbid by long-continued disobedience." This thought derived from his belief that man's senses were formed in accordance with the all-embracing law of evolution from a less perfect to a more perfect state.

William James knew both Spencer and Wundt, but rejected their principles (1890). He theorized that all learning begins in experience, that knowledge comes through an act of consciousness motivated by necessity. Thinking, he said, is made up partly of perception and partly of idea formation. It is an intensely personal thing, highly influenced by emotion. It was James who first offered the 'stream of consciousness hypothesis.'

He said "Objects once experienced together tend to become associated in the imagination, so that when one of them is thought of, the others are likely to be thought of also, in the same order or sequence as before. The laws of motor habit in the lower center of the nervous system are disputed by no one. A series of movements repeated in a certain order tend to unroll themselves with particular ease in that order for ever afterward. Number one awakens number two, which awakens number three, and so on, until the last is produced. A habit of this kind, once become inveterate, may go on automatically. And so it is with the objects with which our thinking is concerned."

Aristotle also described the nature of associative learning and explained the phenomenon of recall in terms of its laws. All psychologists since Aristotle have observed the rule of association by contiguity in time. Popular proverbs also bear out the observations: a burnt child dreads the fire; a person once bitten is twice shy; etc. Berkeley referred to "an habitual and customary connection" between ideas, one being the occasion for the next. Hume wrote of a "gentle force" by which one idea "naturally introduces another" if these ideas have previously occurred together.

James Mill (1829) concurs with these theories: "Our ideas spring up, or exist, in the order in which the sensations existed, of which they are copies. That is the general law of the 'association of ideas,' by which term nothing is here meant to be expressed but the order of occurrence." Mill felt the association of ideas could be either concurrent or successive, and that the association's strength was measurable in terms of its permanence, its certainty and its "facility." He further believed that frequency and vividness determined the strength of an association.

David Hartley (1849) stated that there was physical basis for association of ideas. This physical basis was in the brain, he contended, and the process of association was interlocked with bodily processes and not with ideas alone. He also believed that mental life was composed of sense impressions which left copies of themselves in the form of simple ideas or sensations, and through association, these impressions gained the ability to call up other ideas.

Alexander Bain, an evolutionist and contemporary of William James, described (1855) behavior in terms of reflex and instinct. He noted that "Actions, Sensations and States of Feeling, occurring together or in close succession, tend to grow together, or cohere, in such a way that, when any one of them is afterwards presented to the mind, the others are apt to be brought up in idea." Bain was interested in determining the conditions of learning. He would have liked to be able to explain retention as a neurological process rather than as a mental function.

A pioneer in objectivity, Edward L. Thorndike, the father of the theory of "connectionism" (1914), believed that simple association was not enough to insure future connection, but that a desirable effect was necessary to confirm it. His concept was that there must be contiguity, that if ideas act together they make up another intelligible association, and we then have a stimulus and response association. The hypothesis from which he started was that a neural bond was formed. He conducted experiments to find out by what forces the learning process was conditioned when it was regarded as a connecting of bonds. Among his conclusions was the conviction that the learner's response to a given stimulus—other things being equal—depends upon the "strength of the connection" between them. Thus, the importance of 'stamping in' in learning.

Thorndike listed numerous laws to state his theory. The Law of Effect states that, through use, the neural bonds are strengthened but that painful association decreases their strength.

The Law of Exercise states that a modifiable connection increases the strength, the lack of such connection will decrease strength.

The Law of Readiness deals with motivation and the explanation that it is satisfying to the subject to conduct when the conduction unit is ready.

The Law of Multiple Response describes trial and error learning.

The Law of Attitudes, Dispositions and 'Set' claims that these conditions affect learning.

The Law of Partial Activity points out that there is a choice of elements that will lead to the aim.

The Law of Assimilation or Analogy states that the response is adapted from the experiences of the past.

The Law of Associative Shifting derives from study of the conditioned response.

Thorndike later offered an altered Law of Exercise which stated that mere repetition was not enough to insure learning, but that the degree of satisfaction involved must be given much importance. He also changed the Law of Effect to state that reward strengthens the connection, but punishment weakens it very little.

Further, as an argument against the Gestaltist, who declared that patterns are the basis of the learning process, Thorndike described the "spread or scatter" phenomenon. Each connection, he said, affects all the other connections, past or future, according to satisfaction. He based this explanation on biological foundations.

Another law had to do with Transfer of Learning and stated that a successful response could be gained to a new stimulus, if this new stimulus was similar to a past one. Since learning is transference, adjustments are possible and further learning can take place.

Recent research tends to discount Thorndike's theory of neural bonds, but much of what we accept today about learning still rests on his theoretical structures. There is little argument with his pronouncement that:

> It is the first principle of education to utilize any individual's original nature as a means of changing him for the better . . . All schemes of improving human life must take account of man's original nature, most of all when their aim is to reverse or counteract it.

An interesting postscript for our purpose is that Thorndike considered his laws of learning applicable to animals as well as humans. At least one sleep-learner felt the same way—the man who taught his parakeet its huge vocabulary.

Another school of thought about how we learn is

that of conditioning. Its belief is that the nervous system is the basis of conditioning. This theory is a continuation of Ivan Pavlov's studies of the physiology of learning. Pavlov's experiments, with his celebrated dogs salivating at the sound of a bell, showed that conditioning can bring about reflexive responses to stimuli other than the originally effective ones. The conditioned reflex is explained as being the result of impulses traveling along the brain's neurons in chain fashion and creating a "reflex arc."

John B. Watson espoused behaviorism (1925) and asserted that learning is a simple matter of stimulus and response. For example, fear is learned or unlearned. It is a simple matter of conditioning.

E. B. Guthrie (1952) developed Bain's idea of contiguity. He held that: "A combination of stimuli which had accompanied a movement will on its recurrence tend to be followed by that movement." For him response is divided into movement (motor and glandular phenomena) and act (class of movements expressed through results). He sees learning as action as the result of repetition. He finds that a combination of movement helps to bring about the response, and Guthrie writes, "Effective practice is conducted in the general situation in which we desire the future performance to be given." Logically then, Guthrie would understand that sleep-learners would well be able to recall what they have learned while asleep.

Guthrie felt that forgetting is the inhibition of a response by a competing one, that habit-formation is linked to successful acts and that motivation affects the process since the last response modifies the situation and makes learning possible. This coincides with the rote-learning-plus-motivational approach of the sleep-study school.

Clark L. Hull (1943) formulated a system of behavior highlighted by the principles of habit-formation. He stated that the value of habits is dependent on their usefulness to the individual.

In Hull's system, feeling and consciousness are not of great importance. He makes no distinction between emotional and other forms of behavior. In his careful mathematical description of human functioning, everything is behavior.

In his later work, Hull stated that "learning is a process by means of which the vertebrate individual survives in a world characterized by needs."

The keynote to his explanation of learning is reinforcement and his theory is founded on order and arrangement. Learning is the means by which the organism comes to perceive its world, through the stimuli to its neurological structure. Thus, in Hull's view of habit-formation, learning is conditioning-planning for proper responses, and need is the one for action. Drive gives direction to the response, satisfaction of need leads to reinforcement of stimulus-response connections.

Hull's students Dollard and Miller, carrying on the idea that human behavior is learned, say that maladjustment is a manifestation of inadequate learning, for which we can no doubt substitute inadequate conditioning. In this connection, we are reminded again of Huxley's *Brave New World* and the responsibilities of the promoters of sleep-study and sleep-therapy.

If the behaviorists are right, the speculation arises

that perhaps all of humanity could be beautifully ad justed into an appalling uniformity.

Norbet Wierner, author of *Cybernetics,* attempts to relate human beings' learning mechanisms to the workings of electronic calculators, speaking of the feedback principle, which "means that behavior is scanned for its result, and, that the success or failure of this result modifies future behavior." This implies an integrating process measuring success and failure which will decide the response.

B. F. Skinner (1932) observed behavior and examined habit-building in order to find laws of behavior. The strength of the reflex was his basis of measurement. Although he did not use equations, he too devised numerous laws, including one measuring a threshold of stimulus intensity below which there is no response; one which indicated a latent period between stimulus and response varying with the intensity of the stimulus; one which describes responses persisting after the stimulus has ended, and one which states a similar effect when a stimulus is prolonged as when the intensity of the stimulus is increased. These are the static laws. He also lists dynamic laws of reflex strength: the law of the refractory phrase, stating that the strength of the reflex is low or zero immediately after it has been evoked; the law of reflex fatigue, stating that the strength of the reflex diminishes during repeated elicitation, and returns facilitation, which states that a second stimulus which not capable by itself of eliciting a response, may increase the strength of a reflex; and the law of inhibition, which is that a second stimulus which has no other relation to the effector involved may decrease the strength of the reflex.

Skinner too denies emotions and sees the laws of behavior as existing independently. Perception comes about through the reduction of drives. The effective stimuli lead to reinforcement of the desired response, and repetition or prolongation is all to the good.

The Gestalt explanation of learning stems from the premise that every phenomenon of nature is a whole, not merely a sum of its parts. This whole is the Gestalt. The whole is, in fact, greater than the sum of its parts. Everything is seen in relation to its background, as a figure within a framework, and it is the framework that gives meaning to the figure. We learn in patterns, not in separate parts. Each experience initiates a trace process, and in a different part of the brain there already exist traces which are the results of previous experience. These traces represent two different phases of learning. This system is held to obey the laws of organization. The interaction of traces results in an adjustment of forces, and the organization is continually changing to expand desirable Gestalts.

In time, the Gestaltists say, the compound trace organization transcends individual experiences and may influence their acceptability. Memory is a process by which the traces in the brain undergo certain changes. Rote-memorizing is a conditioned reflex technique, but understanding—apprehending relations, insight, etc.— makes recall more effective.

The Gestaltists say there is essential unity in perception, that "form" in experience is grounded in the physical world. Their claims are that intellectual processes operate as a whole organism responds in a unified way from beginning to end in the learning process; that the organism reacts to total situations and proceeds from the whole to the part and from the general to the specific (the assumption again is that the whole is always greater than the sum of the parts); and that the learning process is one of reorganization—in other words, of forming proper Gestalts.

Motivation is considered important, along with the concept of the whole. This school of thought is a revolt against the stimulus-response interpretation of learning. They deny vehemently that reflexive action is the basis of learning, and find association too mechanistic. It is the quality of the experience, they claim, that makes the experience intelligible.

The process of learning, then, according to the Gestaltists, is one of perpetual patterning. Learning occurs when a stimulus pattern is perceived along with its significance for tension reduction. Forms of behavior which are consistent become part of habit responses. The major concern is with personality and integration.

One of the versions of the Gestalt school is Raymond H. Wheeler's "organismic" learning, which combines energy and subjective designations. Learning is measured in terms of reduction of tension and personality development, and improvement is "at the level of conscious behavior"; it is not merely a result of conditioning, but a result of the relationship between the stimulus pattern and the learner's level of insight.

A theory of purposive learning is presented by Edward C. Tolman (1932). He too is preoccupied with behavior and the need for adaptation. His theory is based on association of stimulus situations with concepts, perceptions and expectancies. He is more concerned with achievement than with the means of achievement. He accepts the ideas that associations occur as a result of contiguity of stimulus pattern and perception or cognition, but he is most interested in the nature and complexity of the response. He describes six kinds of learning:

cathexes, "the acquisition of a connection between a basic drive like hunger and a specific type of goal object" like a particular food, or a negative drive like fright along with a specific object of fear,

equivalence beliefs, "a connection between a positively cathected type of goal—and a sub-goal," or the equivalent negative,

field expectancies, once called "sign-Gestalt expectation," the acquisition by the organism of "sets" or "field expectancies" on successive experiences in a particular environment which makes possible short cuts or roundabout routes,

field cognition modes, meaning that field expectant is dependent not only upon memory but on perception and inference as well,

drive discriminations, the ability to distinguish between different drives,

motor patterns if learned (conditioned) when the patterns lead to the desired goals.

Tolman sees goals and configurations in a cause-and-effect sequence. The social environment is the stimulus, and rewards are of great importance. Practice leads to acquiring the "feel" of the situation.

Norman Maier (1931) offers a theory of frustration along with an explanation of learning. He found that frustration tended to freeze or fixate a response, even if punishment was the ultimate result of the response. He concluded that frustration is an aspect of behavior completely separate from learning. He divides learning into two categories, associative and selective, the first in terms of conditioning, the second in terms of the learning what happens in the course of solving a puzzle, where the outcome provides the direction of the learning. Behavior can be altered in four ways, he says: in the "extension of a response (conditioning) so that it will be expressed in a variety of situations," in changing the consequences of an action; in a "change of perception or stimulus interpretation"; and in "insightful problem solving" in which the goal influences the nature of the insight and resulting behavior (this differs from trial-and-error learning in that insight rather than past experience directs the solving of the problem.

Maier describes behavior changes as: stimulus-response reactions "determined by neural connections only," motivated behavior; and frustration, not guided by consequences but able to be changed by guidance, possibly because of associations acting through neural connections, and in this explanation the fixation response appears to be similar to association by contiguity.

A dynamic approach known as functionalism has been offered by F. S. Robinson. The factors which he considers important in learning are contiguity, assimilation (meaning that one activity prompts another), frequency and intensity. He too is concerned with adaptation, and his interpretation of the mind is based on neural action. Man's intellect causes movements in the direction of adjustment, and environment is a major factor. Practice is extremely important, according to this theory, but operational personality factors are not considered.

Thorpe and Schmuller (1954) have attempted to draw from all of these theories a flexible, integrated understanding of the principle of learning. Searching for a definition, they find that, stated simply, learning is a form of behavior in the acquisition of facts, that it is a social and educational process involving both heredity and environment, and then they go on to suggest as an acceptable statement that "Learning . . . (is) . . . the total changes which occur in an individual as a result of his responses to representative stimuli, present or past. This definition includes the formal aspects of learning of one kind or another which take place throughout the span of life." They believe that there is a relation between personality and the stimulus-response role of learning. Noting that all the theories of learning in acceptance today have grown out of scientific movement and have been experimentally verified, and noting also that individuals vary from the accepted norms, they suggest principles of learning drawn from all schools of thought. These include motivation, adjustment to the level of maturation, pattern learning (the importance of meaningful relationships), evaluation of progress satisfactory personality adjustment, and social growth.

John Dewey saw learning as an experience, and was concerned with the integration and use of knowledge, His theory has been described as problem solving. Adding the social environment to the individual physical apparatus, as equally important to the process of learning, he looked forward to a time when this process would be one in which the functions of the human organism are used in such a way as to make learning socially effective.

It can now be demonstrated that the theory and practice of sleep-learning basically coincide with the accepted theories of the psychologists of learning. In both theories, major stress is given to the primary needs in learning of repetition, reward, motivation and association. Indeed, the direct approach of sleep-learning utilizes these basic concepts to a much more valuable degree than heretofore possible in the science of learning.

chapter V

Validation

Perhaps one way of testing the validity of sleep-learning claims is to compare their consistency with the results of the careful experimentation conducted by the leading psychologists of learning. If they coincide, we can assume there is, at the very least, considerable validity in the sleep-study technique.

What would the ancient Greeks have said? Socrates might have doubted that awareness of universal truth could become a meaningful part of man by virtue of his hearing the refrain repeated during his sleep. Plato might have had similar doubts although both would probably have embraced the opportunity to increase their knowledge.

Aristotle noted the frequent recollection of what is frequently thought about, apparently setting the pace for the stress on repetition. He also said, "it is a fact that there are some movements, by a single experience of which, persons take the impress of custom more deeply than they do by experiencing others many times; hence upon seeing some things but once, we remember them better than others which we may have seen frequently."

And what do the sleep-learning people claim? They find that, once the barriers are overcome, it takes relatively few hours to memorize a play, a whole book of notes or a foreign language. They also find that repetitition is useful. So learning in one's sleep carries with it the same contradictory qualities as conscious learning. Some things require frequent repetition and some are remembered almost immediately. Fewer repetitions are necessary during the Transitional Sleep Period than during the Reverie Period. Sleep-learners can no more explain these phenomena than could psychologists since the days of Aristotle. They can only verify the findings.

Thus we find consistency—even if it is in contradiction.

The early thinkers who stressed the importance of perception through the senses were undoubtedly speaking of perception during waking hours. Here, too, sleep-learning has a common point since it is through the sense of hearing that the subject learns during sleep.

The physiological methods and careful measurement of results, can be considered one of the forerunners of sleep-teachers. While the final answer has not been found, and the successful results can be explained only partly by science, it must be acknowledged that the sleep-learning investigators are attempting to interpret and apply the evidence they have gathered in the light of present scientific knowledge and discoveries.

The theories of association-learning do not appear to be applicable to sleep-learning. The advantage of understanding the material and thinking about it intelligently during waking hours is stressed, but no importance is given to the connections between ideas and facts.

On the other hand, the ideas of reflex and succession, of "stamping in," of the importance of motivation, of the conditioned response, of the positive effects of reward (real and anticipatory) and of recognition of individual differences all crop up in sleep-learning literature.

Trial-and-error learning seems to have no place in what we learn and absorb while asleep. Nor is there any concern with the theory that transference of successful responses makes further learning possible, except that once the barrier is broken, the capacity to sleep-learn expands.

From the reports of how sleep-learning is used in Russia, there can be no doubt that it owes much to discoveries of the conditioning school of adherents as an explanation of how we learn. Once again there is agreement with those who find that motivation and success affect the learning process and that reward strengthens it. There is also agreement that forgetting is inhibition of the response (or learning) by a competing response (or information).

The sleep-therapy approach appears consistent with the behaviorists in that both seem to feel that reinforcement of stimulus-response habits, if they are useful, will make for a happy adaptation to environment; and neither seems to require special consideration of feelings, emotion or consciousness except in terms of behavior.

It must be noted that responsible sleep-learning advocates recognize that problems exist where sleep-therapy alone is inadequate.

What sleep-learning appears to have in common with purposive learning is the importance of achievement and rewards.

From the layman's point of view, there is a good deal of hair-splitting from one school of learning to another. We find highly technical terms, obscure language of specialists and convincing arguments behind every theory. Thorpe and Schmuller's attempt to state principles of learning which are flexible and drawn from all schools of thought appears to be the best solution, the one most likely to consider all proven factors and to result in a balanced, unbiased view.

They include motivation as an important factor. This is stressed in sleep-learning. They are concerned with mature adjustment. So is sleep-learning. They consider pattern-learning and meaningful relationships as basic. This, too, coincides with the advice of sleep-learners.

Evaluation of progress is deemed important. This is a major aspect of the appeal of sleep-learning. Satisfactory personality development and social growth are dual goals in traditional learning and sleep-learning.

It is unlikely that Dewey, who was concerned with learning as experience and with the importance of the social environment, would have been enthusiastic about sleep-learning. He was less interested in the acquisition of facts than in the integration and use of the knowledge acquired. Perhaps the ultimate answer is a careful combination of the advantages of sleep-learning and the conscious use of understanding—which, in fact, is strongly advocated in the printed instructions of sleep-learning.

On the whole, there appears to be considerable evidence that the methods of sleep-learning are to a great degree in accord with the views of the psychologists of learning.

chapter VI

The Mind at Work

It may be possible, when a great deal more is known about the tape recorders in our brains, that we will be able to evaluate the theory which finds a parallel between the human learning process and the activity of the "thinking machines."

We could point out that sleep-learning information is fed to the human mind by machine in a reversal of the familiar feeding of data into a machine by a human. In the first instance, the human can select the information to be given. In the latter, the machine dips into its memory bank to furnish information.

The importance of repetition in sleep-study is easily evidenced by the research work being done by the purveyors of sleep-learning and its related equipment. They have found that the three basics for successful sleep-learning belong in no special order of importance: motivation, understanding of the study material, and repetition.

The Self-Development Research Foundation, which

conducts research in the technique, and publishes periodic research bulletins on test studies, offers conclusive appreciation that the "most successful sleep-study messages are recorded by either the sleep-student, or someone with whom they are familiar." The conception seems clear and logical. In order to learn, awake or asleep, we must have some "reason" or "need" to learn. This is, of course, the motivation. Who then, is better equipped to impress the need, or motivation, than the student himself?

Statements on the tape are always highly affirmative, and delivered in a calm, reassuring voice. This is in accordance with most theories of learning. The old adage about leading a horse to water holds true in every human action. The student will learn when he knows he wants to learn, and why. In addition the repetition of the message deeply imprints the study material into the mind. With the reinforcement of repetition, there is the promise of the reward of successful learning.

It should be understood that the subject really believes the message. The positive conditioning is particularly effective in view of the fact that there is so much negative thinking in the constant "no, no" and "don't" that each child hears in the course of growing up. It seems that the ability to be self-sustaining and independent is built in as a natural human characteristic, but is "worn down" over the years by adult supervision. The impression that almost everything desirable and gratifying is forbidden is a common heritage, indeed. And so the basic idea behind development material to be recorded for sleep-study is the need to negate this previous conditioning with the promise of reward coupled with positive affirmations.

How the affirmations should be stated is a matter which the individual should decide. In some instances, it seems the direction to the subconscious should be for immediate action; in others, forward steps by degrees. The following are examples which have been successfully used:

1. From this moment forth, I shall have an intense dislike for alcohol. The slightest taste of alcohol in any form will make me violently sick. I shall become sick from even the smell of alcohol. Because of this, I shall never taste alcohol again. Before very long, the desire and need for alcohol will disappear completely. I know that I have the power to withstand the temptation to drink . . . AND I WILL NEVER DRINK ALCOHOL AGAIN!

2. I am, by degrees, acquiring an extreme dislike for alcohol. Slowly, but very surely, the taste or even the smell of any form of alcohol will nauseate me. Before very long I will become violently sick at the taste of alcohol and I will lose all desire to ever drink again. By degrees I will accomplish this and . . . I WILL NEVER TAKE ANOTHER DRINK AS LONG AS I LIVE.

The "by degrees" advocates claim that nothing ever occurs instantaneously and that a direct approach might possibly create a subconscious conflict. The conception is that the "habit" was not formed in a short space of time, and it would be more advantageous to slowly condition the mind to accept the message for permanent learning of the material. The conception that the elimination of one so-called "bad" habit will necessarily cause the appearance of a new even possibly more damaging one seems based on mere fiction. Psychologically it is sound that it be understood that we replace the condition we wish to eliminate with the pride of accomplishing the feat. In other words, replacement of the need for alcoholics with the pride of eliminating this supposed "need."

Although there are no established patterns of techniques for recording the wanted material, there is available through testing, the basis for preparation of these messages. The Self-Development Research Foundation in its studies has covered a great variety of subject material that aids the sleep-student in the preparation of his own sleep-study message. They stress that: "Since it is clearly understood that, for any successful learning, both intelligent understanding of the material, and the motivation for wanting to learn the material are of equal importance, Research Bulletins are under two headings: the first is Explanation—which will state the facts on the subject in order that there be clear understanding. The section following is Technique which will be the suggested phrasing for recording the message on this particular subject."

The subject material on the research studies from S.D.R.F. are varied and thorough. We have permission from them to include the following series of studies.

subject: ROTE LEARNING

explanation

Rote learning may be defined as learning through mechanical memorizing, without primary attention to principles, rules, and meanings. This is not to say that rote learning results in learning a set of facts without learning the meaning of these facts; it means only that *during the process of learning* one concentrates entirely on the data to be learned, and not on their meaning. After something has been learned by the technique of rote learning, the meaning of knowledge thus gained will emerge into conscious awareness without further effort on the learner's part.

What, on the basis of available evidence, are the conditions for the optimum acquisition of knowledge? First of all, and most importantly, attending to the material to be learned is not enough; it must be attending *with the intent* to learn it. Secondly, the learner must make sure that he knows the results of his practice by checking his accomplishment from time to time. By knowing how he is getting on, the learner is enabled to check on his right and wrong procedures and so more rapidly select the one and eliminate the other. Thirdly, the principle of rewards must always be kept in the foreground. By keeping the fruitful consequences of his to-be-acquired learning always in mind, the learner will be spurred to persevere in his efforts. This principle

59

reinforces his original motivation for undertaking the learning effort in the first place.

After these theoretical requirements have been fulfilled, the learner will do well to consider the following practical recommendations: (1) *Distributed learning* is more effective than *massed learning*. A great many researchers have found that in learning economy is found by spacing the practice instead of attempting to get it completely formed at one sitting. (2) Rhythm is of great value in the learning process. By adopting a constant rhythm, memorizing will be accelerated. It is no accident that children, when they have to learn to "speak a piece," will instinctively fall into the "sing-song" manner of memorizing. Those who record their own material for sleep-learning must particularly keep this in mind.

Rote learning capacity is not subject to age differences. Thorndike has proved conclusively that learning capacity at age 45 is approximately that of age 16. It is the consensus of research in this area that no one should restrain himself from learning because of a belief or fear that he is too old to be able to learn it.

technique

Record the required information on your Audio Educator Cartridge. If possible, when reading the material to be learned onto the cartridge, attempt to form a rhythm to the material. Do not attempt to absorb an excessive amount of material at once. The processes will best be hurried slowly. It would be beneficial if you were to note on the tape your motivation for wanting to learn this material. Speak slowly and distinctly when recording. When the initial information has been absorbed, continue then to the next.

subject: HABITS

explanation

Habits are determining factors of such weight in human behavior that they could be considered to be forces in themselves. As long ago as 1785, Thomas Reid, the great Scottish philosopher, said: "I conceive (habits) to be a part of our constitution that what we have been accustomed to do, we acquire not only a facility, but a proneness to do on like occasions." In 1872, Alexander Bain gave a vivid description of habits: "The accustomed routine of life leads to a craving almost of the nature of appetite. As the time comes round for each stated occupation, there is a tendency to proceed with that occupation, and an uneasiness at being restrained. Our appetites may have their times of recurrence *determined by our customary periods of gratifying them.*"

We all know that the significance of habits in human life is tremendous. The organization of emotional reactions into habitual forms of activity furnishes stability in human behavior and molds into regular modes of behavior a man's loving and hating, his likes and dislikes, his loyalties, his cynicisms. Character training is actually a process of training desirable attitudes and habits so that socially valuable rather than harmful behavior will be aroused.

The significance of habits can be best brought into focus by pointing out that the compulsive customs of any given society represent the sum total of the habits of the majority of its members. That which a man, his parents, and ancestors have always done determines in large measure his judgments of right and wrong—ethically, economically, politically, and socially.

Naturally, habits are both good and bad. So-called bad habits—such as smoking, drinking, nail biting—are formed much quicker than so-called good habits because they bring more immediate satisfaction, even if their long-range effects are harmful. The development of good habits and the shedding of bad ones is more time-consuming and requires motivation to be achieved. Such motivation must then be supported and fulfilled by persistent learning and in the end (the time invested depends on the individual) it will become a firmly rooted good habit.

technique

Do not attempt the 'blanket' elimination of all undesirable habits at once. Start your program with one habit; after it has been removed, go on to the next. Record the message on your Audio Educator Cartridge in an assured, confident voice; allow the automatic action of the cartridge to repeat the message for your sleep-study periods.

EXAMPLE . . . ". . . I fully understand that I can control myself completely with my mind. . . . I have complete confidence in my ability to stop (name habit) . . . I have trained my mind to accept these suggestions, and I will quickly accept this message and will stop (name habit) . . . I realize I will be a better person for being able to stop (name habit) . . . (* NOTE: emphasize your particular MOTIVATION for wanting to stop this undesirable habit) . . . this will give me great satisfaction . . . everyone will recognize my accomplishment . . . I am proud of my ability to stop (name habit). . . ."

subject: LANGUAGE STUDY

explanation

The knowledge of foreign languages has always been considered the mark of civilized man. Charles V used to say that "the more languages a man knew, he was so many more times a man." According to Goethe, "A man who is ignorant of foreign languages is ignorant of his own," and Roger Ascham, who wrote as far back as the sixteenth century, said that "As a hawk flieth not high with one wing, even so a man reacheth not to excellence with one tongue."

European educators have long concerned themselves with achieving these aims, and in every European country the study of foreign languages is an integral part of school curriculums. The great majority of middle-class Europeans has a working knowledge of at least two languages in addition to his own, and even uneducated Europeans have a better acquaintance with at least one foreign tongue than do most Americans of whatever social class. Americans usually rationalize their ignorance of foreign languages by saying that Europeans have to learn them for simple geographical reasons; dozens of languages are spoken in Europe, and if Europeans are to maintain commercial and cultural contact with one another, they must be able to speak the languages of their neighbors.

While this argument had some merit in the past, when America was separated from the rest of the world by distances that took weeks of travel to cover, it hardly has any validity in an age where geographical distances have become meaningless and where every country in the world is becoming increasingly dependent on every other. At this point in history, it is not merely arrogant to expect the other fellow to learn your language without your making an effort to learn his, but actually dangerous.

Fortunately, concurrently with the ever-increasing advancement in transportation and communication facilities, it is also possible now to learn languages faster and better than it was in the past. Recorded language courses represent a milestone in this area, and the fact that more and more Americans take advantage of them is a hopeful sign for the future.

technique

Any recorded language course that uses the voices of native instructors may be used for sleep-study. It has been determined that language study is accomplished more quickly when the English translation precedes the foreign language. Do not attempt complete mastery of a new language in one night. The accepted technique is to record the English translation of the first two lessons from the instruction manual which is normally included with the recorded language courses; then record the foreign language equivalent from the record, immediately following the English reading. The lesson will be automatically repeated by the Audio Educator Cartridge. As the first lessons are learned, continue to the next, following the same procedure.

subject: TENSIONS

explanation

As Rudyard Kipling said, "I never made a mistake in my life; at least never one I couldn't explain away afterwards."

This explaining to oneself is required as a defense. Tension is an inherent ability of our conscious and subconscious, and, as such, cannot be completely eliminated. However, understanding of the signs of coming tension does prepare us to combat it.

Clinical observations have established that tension is an alarm warning of the approach of fear. External pressures may have been the stimulus, but tensions arise from within ourselves. The condition of tension results from inner conflict. The body actions are controlled by the mind, and the stimulus of tension can cause very real physical manifestations.

Tension then, stems from subconscious conflicts, and since no one is free of these, they must be accepted as part of our lives. Dr. Edmund Bergler in his studies states, "These inner conflicts are closely and unconditionally connected with reproaches of the inner conscience." In reply to the consideration that there is a strong need for unconscious appeasement, Dr. Bergler notes that, "There is a standard technique of unconscious appeasement. It consists of two steps. First, the 'defendant' produces an inner alibi to 'prove' his alleged innocence." Dr. Bergler states that the second step is to rationalize the action thereby offering the necessary excuse that will be accepted emotionally.

The combat of tension is therefore highly personal. It is dependant upon the individual ability to understand many conditions and considerations, and then develop the ability to combat them.

Initially, it is necessary to appreciate that; though we are equipped to control our actions, outside influences supply you with hundreds of nuisances daily. It is through this understanding that it is possible to neutralize these influences. Understand that the actions of others are not contrived as an assault upon you personally; realize that as humans we are subject to the constant reproaches of our inner conscience; attempt to determine how many of your tensions are self-created. Fully appreciate that the nuisances of daily life can be relegated to the category of incidental occurrences, and in the complete picture they will have small influence on the coloration of your life. It must always be understood that we have the inherent ability to control our emotional needs and wants. This ability gives us the understanding that will enable us to control our tensions.

technique

Record the message in a firm voice, using words familiar to you. Allow the message to repeat during sleep-study periods until it is learned.

EXAMPLE: ". . . . I am well aware of the little nuisances that attempt to invade my life . . . and . . . I understand that these intrusions cannot affect the natural progress of my life. . . . I understand and appreciate my abilities to control my tensions by understanding them. . . ."

subject: SELF-IMPROVEMENT

explanation

It has been said that failure in an endeavor does not occur because of inability to handle a problem; it occurs because we do not recognize the problem.

In his autobiography, Benjamin Franklin notes that he tried for many years to improve himself, with no success. Then, one day he listed clearly on paper what he felt to be his problems. This led to his decision to work on one problem at a time, rather than attempt a general self-improvement program. He stated that by following this procedure, he was able to eliminate a good many of his shortcomings in less than a year.

Clear definition of the problem must be established. From this point logic and intelligence direct you easily to a solution. It is obvious that a great opportunity of success exists if we rebuild the wall of our personality one brick at a time.

There are basic facts to be accepted. Just as you 'learned' habits or actions, you must now 'unlearn' them. However, since many of these habits were formed in our youth, they have had many years to develop; they cannot be eliminated overnight. However, no matter how deep-rooted they may seem, you are well-equipped to eliminate them in maturity because of your ability to intelligently recognize the 'need,' or motivation. By the same token, the elimination of habits in children is simplified because they are extremely impressionable, and the habit pattern has not yet become deeply ingrained.

In order to effect successful self-improvement, you must initially determine that you are equipped to handle the 'problem.' You must appreciate yourself. You must then have a substantial 'need' or motivation to accomplish this purpose. The motivation which only you are able to determine, will give you the power and desire to progress.

Since we must share this world with others, it is also important that you recognize the needs and wants of others. We all want recognition and success . . . in varying degrees. Psychologists tell us that if you have little regard for yourself, not only can you not expect others to feel differently about you than you yourself do, but it is also impossible to feel any emotional empathy for others. Understanding then, includes others as well as yourself.

technique

Remember that the best results are accomplished when you concentrate on one 'improvement' at a time. Do not use general language; define the 'problem' clearly. Record the message on your Audio Educator Cartridge in a quiet, firm, persuasive voice; allow the automatic action of the cartridge to repeat the message for your sleep-study periods.

EXAMPLE. . . . I understand that I am equipped to control my actions . . . I can stop (here clearly name the problem) . . . I have complete confidence in my ability to stop (problem) . . . I have trained my mind to accept my suggestions, and I will quickly accept this message because I fully realize I shall be happier for it, and I shall be a better person for being able to control myself by stopping (problem) . . . my accomplishment will give me great satisfaction, and everyone will recognize my

ability to control myself . . . I am proud of this
ability.

subject: MEMORY

explanation

A good memory is a natural function of the
mind; in fact, the act of forgetting is similar to
the act of remembering. It is the subconscious need,
the motivation to remember that is required for
constant, beneficial memorizing. All daily experiences are recorded in our subconscious; every action
noted by the five physical senses makes its impression on the mind.

The 'remembering' part of memory is in our
subconscious; this is our bank, the storehouse of
information that is called upon as required by the
conscious mind. The 'forgetting' part of memory
is in the conscious mind. This is logically understandable, since, if we were to crowd our conscious
mind with the accumulation of our years of gathered information, the required sifting process would
be tremendous. For this reason, the mind brings to
attention only the information required, as it is
needed.

The subconscious mind will absorb information
and daily impressions, and by association, return
the information to the conscious mind when it is
called for. Permit the mind to accept vivid impressions of everything you wish to remember. Associate the new material you wish to remember with

some situation or condition you have already learned. The physical senses are to be utilized: sight, hearing, smell, taste and touch. Extremes will quickly impress the memory: beauty or ugliness; discordant or extremely harmonious sound will be remembered; pleasant or unpleasant tastes will make a distinct impression; odors will leave a definite mark on the memory; objects and surfaces that are harsh and disagreeable or pleasant and agreeable will make a strong impression. Active interest will quicken your ability to remember, and this interest must have your full concentration.

technique

(record on your Audio Educator Cartridge in a quiet, firm, persuasive voice . . . allow the automatic action of the cartridge to repeat the message for your sleep-learning periods)

". . . I understand that I have a good memory . . . I can . . . I will . . . and do have a keen and alert memory. . . . I have complete confidence that my memory will serve me as I need it. . . . I clearly understand the reasons for a good memory, and I know I have everything I need for a good, dependable memory. . . . I have trained my mind to be keen, accurate and dependable. . . . I know that my senses of sight . . . hearing . . . taste . . . smell and touch are all important to my memory and I use each of these senses to make clear, vivid and permanent impressions on my mind. . . . I concentrate on what I wish to remember . . . I have learned to associate new ideas and impressions with ideas and impressions previously learned. . . . I know that I have an accurate and dependable memory. . . . I use my memory constantly during my work . . . and also for my pleasure . . . and I am proud of my memory, and of my control of my memory. . . . I have a good memory. . . . I . . . have . . . a good memory."

subject: RELAXATION

explanation

The concept of relaxation is the product of our industrial civilization. Before the advent of the Industrial Revolution life was unhurried; such notions as time, tensions, and anxieties were purely abstract and occupied the attention of philosophers only. After the machine entered the scene and Western Civilization began to focus all its energies on the production of goods, there developed an entirely new array of human problems, all of which were related, in one way or another, to the problem of pressures. Western man who for a thousand years knew only the periodic pressures of war and disease was suddenly confronted with the fact that he has traded in his long-accustomed tranquility for the milliard pressures that are the by-products of material progress.

Consequently, a way had to be found for man to periodically turn away from the frantic hubbub of progress and thus renew his energies and creative potentials. Relaxation—from the Latin word meaning "to loosen, to detach"—soon occupied the attention of psychologists, industrial time-study researchers, and medical workers; for to be properly utilized it had to be understood first. It was found that anxieties, worries, and tensions manifested themselves physically in the symptom of muscle tension, and if muscle tensions could be relaxed, their original cause would be relieved, resulting in the state of mind popularly referred to as relaxation.

It is now generally recognized that tensions are not the results of overwork but of overworry; it is not the actual act of working but its by-product, worry, that causes muscle tensions. Consequently, the art of relaxation must be focused on the individual's emotional apparatus. It is a well-established psychological fact that the subjective state of an individual—the way he feels—is a function not only of his physiological state (muscular, neural, endocrinal, etc.) but also of his thinking process. Therefore, the aim of a relaxation period is twofold: on the one hand, one must concentrate on dissolving muscle tensions, and on the other hand, one must suspend worry-centered thinking. It is easy to see, that by accomplishing the first, one will have accomplished the second as well.

technique

The aim is to suspend the mind from worry. This is most easily accomplished by causing the mind to concentrate on a subject away from the tensions that caused the condition. The following example should be recorded on your Audio Educator Cartridge in a soft, persuasive voice. Speak very slowly . . . but with assurance.

EXAMPLE: "As I lie here I feel comfortable . . . I feel the muscles in my feet loose and weightless . . . this pleasant . . . comfortable feeling is slowly traveling up my legs . . . leaving my muscles loose and relaxed . . . the muscles of my stomach are relaxed . . . my chest and lungs are free to breathe easily . . . the muscles are relaxed . . . the muscles of my back and neck are loose and relaxed . . . my mind is free and uncluttered. . . . I can think only of relaxation. . . . I shall arise when I have decided . . . completely relaxed . . . relaxed."

subject: SMOKING

explanation

Depending on who you are, smoking can be a source of untroubled pleasure, a matter of indifference, a source of irritation, or an obsession. Also depending on who you are, you may not give smoking a thought, you may want to cut down your daily ration, or you may want to give it up altogether. If you get pleasure out of smoking, and you are not bothered by the controversy that is raging over its alleged ill effects, then you have no problem. Your problem begins when and if you decide to cut down your tobacco consumption or give it up.

If you have made such a decision, the first thing to be considered is not *how* to go about it, but *why*.

In other words, you must establish your motivation for your action; you must construct a base for your future restraint. Such motivation varies from person to person: some people decide to give up smoking because they feel that it's harmful to their health; others do it to cut down on expenses. Whatever the motive, it must not only exist, but be strong enough to influence your actions.

Smoking is a habit, and as it was pointed out in a previous Research Bulletin, all habits are acquired. It follows logically that whatever is acquired can also be dispensed with, although it is a matter of fact that uprooting a habit is a far more time-consuming process than acquiring one. Nevertheless, once a sufficiently strong motive for the uprooting process has been established, the actual process becomes merely a matter of time and work.

Sleep-education techniques can be of considerable help in giving up the smoking habit. For example, a man who feels that smoking constitutes a hazard to his health, will do well to enlist the help of his sleep-learning equipment to reinforce that feeling until it's strong enough to make him want to do something about it. It is not enough to repeat to oneself, "I want to give up smoking . . . I want to give up smoking . . . one must say, "Smoking is bad for my health." In that way, the unconscious forces which always operate towards the survival of the organism are aroused, and the desire to give up a habit, which is subconsciously considered harmful, will become irresistible.

The same principle applies even when the motivation is different than that of health. Any motivation considered beneficial by the subconscious will trigger a conscious and willed effort toward achieving that particular benefit.

technique

As in all message recording, record the information with calm assurance. Remember, the confident voice you use in recording the message is the confident voice you will hear during your sleep-study periods.

". . . (your name) . . . you want to stop smoking . . . . you know that smoking is harmful to your good health, and you want to maintain your good health . . . you know that the taste of tobacco is unpleasant . . . you know it is a dirty habit that causes a great deal of inconvenience in addition to restricting your opportunity to a full and complete life . . . you will give up smoking and continue on to a complete and full life. . . ."

subject: OVERWEIGHT

explanation

The subject of overweight has probably occupied more space in periodicals, newspaper columns, as well as on book publishers' lists, than any single nonpolitical one in the last five years. The causes, manifestations, effects, and every possible aspect of overweight have been more than amply discussed, analyzed and commented upon. Nevertheless, the fact remains that even though the harmful and un-aesthetic nature of overweight has been imprinted upon the public consciousness, the number of overweight people keeps on increasing, and a great majority of those who had been overweight to begin with continue to fight a generally losing battle.

For the purposes of this Research Bulletin the problem of overweight can be simply stated. Aside from those cases where overweight is a result of glandular dysfunction—and such cases belong exclusively within the province of medicine—people who weigh more than they ought to, eat more than they ought to. By cutting down on their food intake, their surplus weight will soon disappear. The only problem, therefore, is the regulation of food intake in order to achieve a healthier state and a more aesthetic appearance.

This, of course, is easier said than done, which is not to say that doing it is inordinately difficult. Again and again, these Research Bulletins have emphasized the crucial importance of motivation in all human affairs, and the problem of overweight is no exception. A sufficiently strong motive for wanting to lose weight must be found if any attempt—whatever the method used—is to be successful. No general formula can be given that will apply to everyone; each individual must search for his own motive—the one, and there is only one, which is significant and meaningful for him. By examining one's hopes, aspirations, and as yet unfulfilled desires, one thing is certain to emerge, *the* one thing that will make losing weight all important, that will override all other considerations and difficulties.

Once the motivation has been established and the forces of the subconscious enlisted in its support through the correctly applied methods of sleep-education, with time and patience overweight will yield to the stronger, healthier instincts of the personality.

technique

The message is to be recorded on your Audio Educator Cartridge in a quiet, firm, persuasive voice. Remember that your particular motivation must be included in the message.

". . . (your name) . . . you want to lose weight because . . . (motivation—i.e., look better, feel better, increased self-confidence, better health) . . . You will eat the right foods to maintain good health; you know what these foods are. You will not eat fattening foods . . . you will find fattening foods distasteful. . . . (your name) . . . you will lose weight and then your appearance will improve . . . you are proud of yourself and your ability to control yourself. . . . you realize that your appearance is important . . . and your increased confidence will open many doors for you . . . doors to happy and successful living. . . ."

subject: ANXIETY

explanation

Our daily lives are comprised of hundreds of impermanences. These very impermanences, by virtue of the fact that we allow them, constantly oppress us and strongly influence our actions. Our anxious concern for our individual welfare, and the condition of factors outside our scope of control, can cause us considerable anxiety that we may be called upon to endure physical or emotional hurt.

The condition of anxiety is rooted deep within the subconscious, stemming most probably from the primeval fears of man. Researched evidence states that anxiety cannot be separated from our lives. Considering this research to be conclusive, we must then train ourselves to accept its natural, expected intrusion into our daily pattern. With logical understanding and observation we can easily learn to 'live with' our anxieties by preparing ourselves emotionally to handle them.

Initially, we must recognize that any rational, functioning person has some built-in anxieties. Allowing these anxious feelings full control can inhibit our progressive actions. Fear, or anxiety that we may fail in an endeavor, can keep us from progressive activity. Understandably, we understand that the pressures of anxiety-failure can be the direct cause of failure. This negative outlook will cause us to restrict our actions and force us into areas that will eliminate the possibility of failure in an action by eliminating the action itself. This flight from reality will offer no competition or the need to prove our natural abilities and talents.

It is important that we understand our inherent anxieties are of use to us. It is these same anxious feelings that protect us in a possible time of danger, as in the simple process of crossing a busy street, or when driving an automobile. We now see that anxiety acts as a warning of consequences for actions.

Primeval man had anxieties restricted to his particular needs. His requirements were basic, food and shelter. Our modern civilization has a great deal more to offer, and it is our need to strive for these achievements that compounds our anxieties. It must, however, be understood that the reward of accomplishment in business and social life greatly surpasses in reward the anxieties faced.

Since we know that anxiety is a natural existent of man, and we understand that we can control these feelings to a great degree, we must now proceed to replace our primeval anxieties with primeval confidence.

technique

Record the message in phrasing that is familiar to you. Allow the repetitive action of the Audio Educator Cartridge to repeat the message during sleep-study times until it has been learned.

EXAMPLE: ". . . . I am completely aware of my natural abilities to control my actions. I am confident in my actions . . . and I have no need to escape from my anxious feelings. . . . I can control these feelings because I am confident in my ability . . . and I always use my inherent abilities to the utmost. . . ."

Much of the available material on sales training seems to establish the salesperson in a format of predetermined answers to assured questions the prospect will ask. The correct answers are gone into at great length, and in many cases are expected to be delivered as memorized. Correct posture, personal cleanliness, offensive habits such as smoking are given great importance in many training programs. From this are we then to assume that the successful salesperson is an immaculate, pre-conditioned parrot?

This is not, of course, the case at all. The successful salesman has been proven to be an aggressive personality that has mastered both himself and the psychology of selling. He equips himself to project confidence in himself and his product. Information concerning his product is firmly established in his mind, eliminating the need for concentration on these details and thereby allowing him to exert his capacities on his own personality development and his potential customers' personal needs. He completely understands the need to project his confidence in the product and himself.

The successful salesman understands that the prospect is a member in good standing of the human race, and as such is subject to the same needs and desires as anyone else—including, of course, the salesperson. This leads us to understand that buying and selling are highly emotional. The emotional needs of the prospect must come to favorable grips with the emotional security radiated by the salesperson. The prospect requires assurance that the product will answer his needs; he can best get this assurance from the salesperson.

Negatively, we must appreciate that the buyer who recognizes the lack of self-confidence in the salesperson is forced into an emotional situation where he must also question the product.

From this we can determine that the successful salesperson is well aware of his influence over the buyer, or prospect, and so projects this carefully, self-developed influence. This projection stems from self-confidence—in himself, and in his product and his knowledge of it.

technique

Self-confidence is best initiated with complete knowledge of the product. This is easily handled by recording the product information on the Audio Educator Cartridge and allowing the repetitive action of the cartridge to teach this material during sleep-study times. After the product information has been learned, self-confidence affirmations should then be recorded and learned. The basics of successful projection are:
1. Establish yourself as an individual personality
2. Make your interest in the prospect's needs quickly and easily apparent

3. Assure the prospect by your manner that you are proud of your product and in your ability to sell it.

subject: STUTTERING

explanation

Prior to the late 1940's, the subject of stuttering was shrouded in a cloak of old wives' tales, its nature obscured by an accumulation of ancient superstitions and pseudo-scientific hodge-podge. It was thought to be related to such differing disturbances as those of heart rate, blood pressure, basal metabolic rate, biochemical dysfunctions, and—as it was believed for a long time—left-handedness.

As a result of these erroneous beliefs, people who suffered from stuttering were subjected to a continuously changing barrage of misinformation and misguidance, exposing them to unfounded surges of hope as well as unjustified fits of despair. As late as 1944, the causes of stuttering—in the words of Dr. Harris Hill of the University of Indiana—were "still as distant from discovery as they were 4000 years ago."

Extensive laboratory research and testing during the last fifteen years brought about a remarkable change in the understanding and, consequently, in the cure of stuttering. It is now quite clear that stuttering is not in any way related to, or a result of, constitutional defects, and that there are no organic differences between stutterers and non-stutterers. It is now agreed upon among speech pathologists that stuttering appears to be the result of environmental reactions to patterns of speech formation in early childhood.

Findings on the sources of stuttering resulted in therapeutic advances as well. For example, *it was firmly established that the more a stutterer talks, the better he talks:* an average stutterer will cut the number of stuttered words by about 50 percent after having read a passage aloud five times in succession. Also, it was found that the more listeners a stutterer has, the more he stutters; with few exceptions, stutterers talk perfectly well when they are by themselves. Still another finding of great therapeutic import was the fact that most stutterers will speak perfectly well if they read aloud while receiving very loud sounds through earphones.

The new understanding of the stuttering process makes it possible for stutterers to effect speech improvement even if they have no access to a speech clinic. By talking and reading aloud for a fifteen-minute period into the microphone of a tape recorder, and then playing back the tape, the stutterer is able to observe exactly what he does when he stutters and how he does it. He will become *conscious* of what he does when he stutters, and by conscientious practice his chances of achieving normal speech will be increased considerably. Observation, practice, and self-confidence are the cornerstones of improvement; the first two can be accomplished by applying the findings of speech pathologists, as outlined in this bulletin. Self-confidence will be the natural result of their application.

Discussing the permanence of results of the sleep-study advocates say it depends on the individual's degree of suggestibility and desire to learn the material or to overcome the habit. In the instance of study material, the technique meets little resistance. However, with the elimination of an unwanted habit, it is necessary to eliminate the gratifying immediate pleasures that are available through the repetition of the habit. As is evident, it will take a longer time to break away from the conditioning of previous years toward the eventual elimination of the unwanted habit.

The psychological explanation for the effects of repetition in sleep-therapy which is offered is that:

> Any persistently duplicated or long-sustained repeats of some specific mental picture will eventually bring about vast electronic or submolecular shifts within the body and usually eliminate the roots of the disturbance. As to the suggestibility of the individual, everyone is suggestible to some degree, and by conscientious practice should be able to develop that suggestibility to a degree. Schrenk-Netzing placed the number of persons susceptible to direct hypnosis at 90%, so the incidence of those susceptible to indirect suggestion should run substantially higher, probably 99%.

Repetition is also used to induce relaxation and receptivity to the material to be learned. The most accepted method is the use of word pictures to suggest a gradual descent into the lower realms of consciousness. Word pictures vary, but they must always offer a peaceful, gradual descent: using an escalator. . . . descending deeper . . . dee . . . per . . . deeper . . . into pleasant sleep and relaxation. Repetition of the words "deep" and "relax" is constant. A progression of movement is used, always going "down . . . relaxed . . . ree . . . laxed . . . dee . . . per . . . dee . . . per." The vivid impression necessary in the induction can be a word picture of decending a staircase, step by step; relaxing on a couch or bed as it slowly descends into the realm of sleep and subconscious receptivity.

It is apparent that the sleep-learning approach is, in many ways, consistent with the principle of hypnosis. Stress is laid on the importance of relaxation, on creating a favorable emotional attitude, on the power of suggestion and in the use of repetition.

We can now investigate sleep-learning in the light of present knowledge and theories about suggestion.

chapter VII

Suggestion

Since the progressive development of learning is, in a great many instances, involved with the basic principles of suggestion, it follows then that we should further define suggestion.

In the broad definition, we must concern ourselves with the two basic forms of suggestion. The first we shall call the "definite suggestion" which in effect demands immediate action on the suggested material. This is more easily illustrated by a campaigner for political office making the definite suggestion that the voters accept him—with the supplied motivation in the form of material or social gains promised to the prospective voter; this, then is a definite action suggestion. The accrued benefits are made clear by the campaigner, leaving no room for the voter to supply the motivation. It is important to note that "suggestions" are not of any value until they are accepted. We will accept this, or any, suggestion, only when we are convinced that the benefits promised are eventually to be placed within our reach through the actions of this candidate. Our individual acceptance of the promises or motivation determines our degree of suggestibility.

Next, we are faced with the gentle, subtle suggestion. The "subtle suggestion" does not demand or require immediate action. Instead, though the same gratification or motivation is offered, the subtle persuader allows you to add to his suggested material, in effect, leads you "into the picture" where you become an active participant in the promised rewards. This is, of course, highly individual, and allows the emotions full play to imagine the benefits you may expect from your acceptance of the suggestion. Prime examples of this are apparent in the advertising which faces us in the periodicals, radio and television. There, in most cases, suggestions are offered in small, easily acceptable doses. Suggestion is the business of the advertising people, and, without entering into its value, we must agree as to its effectiveness. The advertiser fully realizes that the consumer must emotionally achieve a benefit from his product even before buying it. The feeling of well-being that will come from the purchase of the seller's product must be instilled before he, or she, will make the trek to the counter and ask for the specific merchandise. The promise of fulfillment is in every line written, in every complete smile by every complete actor and actress that people the selling commercial or advertisement.

Advertisers understand that "everyone wants to be first . . . second." This is, of course, true. The seller constantly builds an image to the consumers to assure them that they will join the great number of prior users of the product promoted, thereby allowing them to compete favorably with the crowd. This is also a matter of psychological motivation. Suggestion, then, is not a new subject to any of us; we are faced with its positive results every day.

Again, it must be understood that no sugestion has any value unless it is accepted. In *The New York Times* of September 1960, Dr. Theodore X. Barber established that, "Through the power of suggestion, results are possibly comparable with those achieved when trappings of the popularly known 'hypnotism' are used, those for putting the subject 'in a trance.'"

In door-to-door experiments, Dr. Barber found that at least 20% of those approached would act upon direct suggestion. Another 28% of those approached did most of the tests successfully, but finally balked on the whole series. This is further indication of susceptibility to suggestion that is a part of us all. It is interesting to note that the professional lay hypnotist does not claim any supernatural powers for himself. Mrs. Rita Sperling, a New Jersey hypnotherapist, contends that hypnosis, in fact, is nothing more than the accepted suggestion, and the student of hypnosis must be made to understand that as a basic fact. Responsible proponents of suggestive psychology hasten to clarify the many mistaken impressions that have been built upon a foundation of half-facts since the days of Mesmer.

In Hamburg, reports *Variety*, phonograph recordings for patients following analysis, recorded with suggestive therapeutic material for "do it yourself" therapy at home, are available only with a medical prescription at the corner drug store. The idea of the records is the repetition of good, or positive suggestions to help the patient live a better life.

Suggestion is most effective when pre-suggestion conditioning has taken place. This is achieved normally by instilling a feeling of well-being or complete physical and mental relaxation in the prospective receiver of the suggested material. Since the receiving of suggestions is akin to the reception of material to be learned, we can readily understand this since we do most readily accept anything when we are at our most relaxed.

There has been a substantial amount of discussion regarding the similarity between suggestibility in a human and the conditioned reflex that Pavlov demonstrated every time he conditioned a glandular or motor reflex in his dogs. Since there are vast areas that have been untouched in the human mind, no definitive study has yet been offered. However, from the information available, we can assume that the mind can be, and constantly is, conditioned for future activity, by suggestions that have some connection with the conditioned reflex. V. M. Bechterev touched upon the conditioned reflex. He wrote, "Every word, being a sign, is, in accordance with the association-reflex scheme, associated as a secondary stimulus either with an external or internal stimulus, or with some state, posture, or movement of the individual in question. The word consequently plays the role of an external stimulus, and becomes a substitute, according to the association established, for an external influence or a certain inner state."

Andrew Salter feels that parroting suggestions are not necessary to the subject's susceptibility, instead he advocates the "inward thinking and visualizing" of the suggested material.

There are some rules that can be applied to suggestion. However, like many laws, they apply constantly "except when. . . ." The all-decisive factor remains—the human element. We can only approximate human behavioral patterns. We know that the capacity to receive suggestion is inherent in all. The problem remains, how do we offer these suggestions for complete, willing acceptance. To a degree, this also has been determined, but only through trial and error.

It is to be agreed that a positive outlook on the everyday situations we are faced with are most certainly of great benefit to our physical and mental well-being. Whether the cup it "half empty" or "half full" will determine our approach to living. Obviously, the half-full cup is the positive approach. So it is in our daily living needs, the ability to treat each activity as a beneficial, pleasurable experience will add greatly, not only to the individual experience, but also to our general living pattern.

In this manner, we now are made aware that the suggestion will be received, only when there is the promise of a reward. In some cases we find that the "negative suggestion" is accepted more quickly than the positive. It is so in habits; the so-called "bad habit" offers immediate reward, and with this speedy satisfying of our immediate needs, the negative suggestion is accepted. Discernment in the acceptance of a suggestion is wholly dependent upon the individual need. The need will determine the response to the suggestion.

Since we are concerned with suggestion in pertaining to learning in general, and sleep-learning in particular, let us now examine the relationship between suggestion and the established theories of learning.

In exploring the theories of learning, we find that many researchers agree that learning, which includes any learning pattern, either self-induced, or through outside influence, is substantially influenced by the emotions. Since our emotions do control our likes and dislikes, and also determine our needs and motivation toward a situation, we must all agree that we will learn what we wish to learn. Simply put, we will agree to accept the material only after we have decided it will be gratifying to do so. This then, applies to all forms of learning. It must be understood that we had to learn all of our physical and psychological actions and inhibitions. So, though we laboriously placed one foot in front of the other when we learned to walk, we now handle this action subconsciously, without the conscious mind being at all involved. This, then, is also a conditioned habit. It does not require any further development for action. The child must first learn the use of its reflexes and motor ability before it can find its mouth to feed itself; it must also find the strong and powerful emotion of pain and also the pleasurable feeling of security through learning.

As children, we are generally dependent upon outside guidance to lead us to these understandings. As we grow to adulthood, we must then lead ourselves, supplying our own motivation. The ability to learn never leaves us. We understand this. And, since we do, why then, do we not apply ourselves to the accumulation of this material?

There are many reasons. They all return, however, to the desire, or the need to accumulate information. The constant excuses that are available to us are varied as our imagination. The fact of the matter, however, is apparent. If we learn when and what we want to learn, then it follows that we also do not learn because it is our decision. It returns to the original understanding. We will accept the suggestion we want to accept, whether it comes from within ourselves, or from an outside influence.

This seems to indicate that we are capable of establishing a pattern of learning that will be of great benefit to us. But, can this pattern be established by an outside influence? The psychologists say yes, indicating that preparation of material to be learned must take into consideration the emotional need of the learner. The new teaching machines that are now gaining widespread attention are taking into full account our emotional needs in the preparation of the material. The questions are followed by the answers. If the student has correctly answered the question, he will receive instant emotional gratification; if the answer was incorrect, he will then receive the correct reply to the question posed, and thus find gratification through having acquired the knowledge. Of course, good results in anything will lead to better results, and the student who had answered the question correctly will, in most cases go on to more correct answers.

Suggestion plays a strong role in learning. We are, as individuals, the sum of many parts. We have taken the bits and pieces of individuals and situations we have encountered in our lives, offered our own interpretations, and become the personalities we now are. We accepted these daily occurrences as suggestions, and in the most part, our inherent discernment abilities have made us all the better for it.

Now let us relate suggestion to sleep-learning. We have learned that we can, and will, accept material that we want to. This material must offer us the emotional gratification, fill the need, lead us to the motivation we require before we will accept it.

Sleep-learning researchers fully understand this, and take full advantage of these established facts. The sleep-student, in addition to preparing the material to be learned himself, records the message on the tape in his own voice. His emotional need to accept the material is apparent to him, and full advantage is thus taken. The sleep-learner understands that the material he wishes to learn must come to him at a time when he is in the emotional position to accept the material. Though very little is known about sleeping itself, researchers have found that the mind is in constant activity every second of our lives, awake or asleep. The physiological need for sleep is apparent; the elimination of the toxic effects which inhabit our bodies after use requires relaxation and neutralization. The psychologist understands that we condition ourselves to sleep when we lie in a prone position and suggest drowsiness and the relaxing and beneficial results achieved from sleep. There is no established time period, or number of hours arranged for the sleeping period. This, too, is a highly individual thing, and will differ with each person depending upon the physical and emotional requirements.

The sleep-learning people have, through exhaustive

tests, determined an approximation of the sleep-study times. There are still a number of differences of opinion as to the "right" time for sleep-study. However, since very little is actually known of the activity of the mind in sleep, it seems unlikely that a definite decision can be made to determine the correct or most beneficial sleep-learning study periods.

However, in an assessment of the proposed study periods, a form of agreement is reached that some assimilation of the study material takes place during the entire sleep-period. It is, obviously, not necessary to continue the repetition for the entire sleep-period, and agreement seems to be that the two and one-half hour period immediately following going to sleep, and the one and one-half hours prior to awakening will offer the most satisfactory results. The problem seems to be to determine whether the entire sleeping period is needed for sleep-study, or not. Consensus of opinion seems to indicate that the full sleep-time is not needed.

It is of prime importance that the students of both learning methods and psychotherapy are delving as thoroughly as is possible with the limited knowledge available, into the part that suggestion plays in our daily lives. The creative abilities are under question and appraisal. Do we all have the ability for creation and original thinking? If so, can this be developed through teaching methods? If the capacity for forms of creation are inherent in humans can it be brought to effective action through suggestions that will stimulate us toward creativity?

There is little question that each day brings to us new proof of the limitless ability of mankind. The "impossible" is an everyday occurrence. And yet, the greatest part of the growth of man has been out of himself. We are fast taming the elements: nature is being made to work for us; we have reached toward the stars successfully, but very few inroads have been made into the true and complete understanding of man himself. What is our full capacity? We will one day know.

chapter VIII

Memory

What makes us remember? Why do some people have good memories and others poor? Why do we remember some things with ease and find it almost impossible to retain others? Is there a technique of remembering, a trick of association, a gimmick of arrangement? Or is it as simple a matter as remembering what we want to remember, and forgetting what we don't want to remember?

In defining memory, James D. Weinland writes that there is no sharp dividing line between learning and memory, since all learning is based on memory. He makes time the one distinction, in that memory is learning that persists. A memory so ingrained that it requires no effort at all is a habit. Memory is a function of the mind, and greater intelligence and better memory usually occur together.

Memorizing, according to Knight Dunlap, has to do with thinking about as well as of the item. It also has to do with desire to learn, and with persistence. He recommends avoiding constant evaluation of progress; progress should be checked, infrequently. Full attention should be paid to the subject, and added to that, he suggests negative practice—the effort to forget. The reason for negative practice is the theory that effort is detrimental to achievement. So often we are not able to remember something no matter how hard we try, then when we stop trying we suddenly find ourselves remembering. So Dunlap turns it around and says to try to forget, and this effort will get in the way of forgetting.

In the remembering of details, Dunlap says, the purposes behind the remembering must be considered. Is the subject memorizing in order to make use of the details thus acquired or for some trivial purpose? Dunlap is weighing values as well as means in this discussion. He also mentions the importance of personal and social adjustment.

The overall theory behind Dunlap's discussion is that the way of learning lies in the formation of habits. Here we see a similarity to the conditioning theory. But in Dunlap's approach other factors are stressed as equally important. In order to break habits, for instance, it is necessary to understand the situation, to accept the proper ideals, to have a genuine desire to realize these ideals, and to persist in practice aimed at accomplishing the end of the view. There are habits of thought and habits of emotional response. Learning ability, which he calls intelligence, varies, with home influence, social training, basic learning ability and incentive.

Ian M. L. Hunter, in discussing memory, tells us it is easier to recognize then to recall. Among the considerations in determining how quickly we can memorize are meaningfulness, which helps, and the amount of material to be memorized, for as the material increases, the length of time necessary for learning increases disproportionately.

The characteristics of the learner must be considered as well—his emotional state, the deterrent effects of illness, fatigue, drugs or excitement. It is theorized that age affects learning capacities as well. It is claimed that there is a progressively diminishing increase in memory span with the increase of age. Intelligence brings with it high learning efficiency. And speed has values apart from the time-saving aspects: it has been found that a fast learner learns better.

Hunter reports that reading plus recitation results in better learning and remembering than reading alone. The explanation is that the combination of the two involves active participation, provides knowledge of results and increases motivation, and constitutes direct preparation for later recalling. He finds pros and cons in the argument about the whole versus part learning. Both, he concludes, have their uses. Whole learning is good for short pieces, but a combination would be necessary for longer and more difficult material.

Short learning sessions are advised.

The best results are achieved when they are spaced.

Accurate first impressions are extremely important.

Overlearning (review) is recommended, as well as integrating the material.

There is no one cause of forgetting, Hunter states. The reason could be physiological—for instance, a deterioration of the trace, that is, of the organic changes produced by learning; or an actual injury or disease of the brain. Another cause could lie in behavioral processes, which include retroactive interference, altered conditions during remembering, and repression.

It is pointed out that interpretation can affect or distort memory. This accounts for inaccurate witnessing, where the facts reported are the results of observation plus interpretation. This includes on-the-spot interpretation, which happens almost without the observer's awareness, and the subtle changes that occur in the course of thinking about the event later. The memory becomes clouded and colored by myriad influences.

Hunter says the hypnagogic state (Reverie Period) just between waking and sleeping is the time the subject is particularly rich in imagery, which is frequent and vivid.

An interesting point is made about the difference between memory and the use of knowledge. It has been noted that along with the development of skill in abstract thinking there is a decrease in imaging ability. If there is a correlation between imaging ability, as there appears to be, and receptivity in general, are we then, to assume that analytical thinking tends to inhibit the capacity for quick rote memorizing?

This leads to the phenomenon known as photographic memory. Hunter tells us it is an incorrect term, that this term of memory isn't really photographic. It is actually a form of visual imaging, very strong in children, but rare in adults. This capacity is known among the researchers as *eidetic memory*—a high degree of visual imaging, but not totally photographic in that everything that is seen is registered, no matter how irrelevant to the material. Selectivity is involved—something unknown to the camera lens.

Hunter draws a fine line between learning and memory. Little or nothing is known of the physiological process. He lists as efficient techniques of study: selective observing or perceiving, organizing of the material and distributing the effort involved in study, and he rates organizing and finding the underlying principle most effective. Efficient learning, he says, is deliberate and fully conscious—not drill.

The neat little packages of advice offered by memory specialists are the conclusions drawn from the numerous investigations made in the field. Careful experiments have been conducted and the results tabulated and correlated, and from these results certain behavior is concluded to be representative of the process. Since the tests usually involve only a sample group, they cannot be considered absolute proof, but they do indicate a tendency, at the very least. Here is a brief review of some of these investigations.

One of the earliest memory experiments was conducted by Hermann Ebbinghaus at Harvard (1892-93). He came to the conclusion that things heard and seen spontaneously were remembered best. Subsequent experiments did not always bear this out. In some instances variations were found among age groups. Some found hearing more effective, some sight.

In 1912 Henmon noted that most individuals are of the mixed imagery type. But again in subsequent experiments different results were obtained. Wewick tested seventy college subjects in 1932, and found that the auditory mode of learning was superior for them, both for immediate recall and for recall after a delay of from five days to five months.

In 1934 Stanton's experiments bore out this finding,

but not with statistical significance in all cases. In the area of suggestibility, or influencing, Wilke found the audio-visual combination more effective, and since his subjects did not know they were being tested this experiment was more like an actual life situation.

Frank R. Elliot notes that prior to 1932 simple or nonsense materials were used, and in these experiments the results favored the visual over the auditory mode of learning. But since 1932, when larger numbers have been tested, using connected, sense materials, auditory was favored over visual learning. Elliot conducted tests for recall and recognition, using fictitious advertisements. His results showed the highest scores in a combined visual-auditory approach, the next highest for auditory methods, and the third for visual.

In discussing why the best results were obtained when audio and visual stimuli were combined, Elliot states that tests have shown that a summation of stimuli, facilitation, and heightening effects are characteristic of the simultaneous stimulation of two receptor systems. He notes that we hear better when we see as well, and that we see better with a combination of other sense stimuli —auditory, olfactory, and cutaneous. This phenomenon is accounted for by increased activity in the cerebrum. It was found that under combined audio-visual stimuli accuracy improved as well. The visual-auditory approach seems, Elliot finds, to reduce distractions, improve attentions, remove uncertainty, enhance accuracy, and reinforce memory impression.

In its own area, the sound of the human voice has been shown to be of great value. There is social satisfaction involved. Cantrill and Allport found that people prefer, two to one, to hear news on the radio rather than to read it in a paper and nine to one to hear a speech rather than read it. Elliot notes, however, that the role of habit must be considered in this argument of audio versus visual, for people adapt to shifts.

Elliot found that memory was better after broken or serial presentation. The advantage, he concluded, seems to lie in the distribution of learning and in repetition. Another of his conclusions is that education shows in the difference in memory. College groups usually remember more than non-college groups. The explanation offered is that they see more relations and their associational capacities are stronger. Tests to determine the differences in memory capacities between the sexes were inconclusive. In some areas men were shown to remember more than women, but the combined visual-auditory advantage was not so significant for men. The possibilities that women listened to the radio more, or were less well educated, were offered as explanations. The impact of television since these tests were conducted may reveal different results.

Elliot suggests that perhaps the reason for the advantage of audio over visual stimuli lies in the fact that during audio experiences no time is spent examining. The stimulus is received as presented, so there is a more equal distribution of attention.

Early in the century a study of auditory memory consciousness was made by F. Kuhlmann. He used phonograph records to investigate recall of auditory material. As he saw it there were three modes of recall: auditory imagery of the words appeared at once without any process preceding it as an aid to recall; concrete visual magery of the persons and things referred to appeared first as a means of recalling the words; or words were inferred from the contents as already recalled.

Kuhlmann found that the character of auditory imagery varied with reference to the completeness with which the sentence was recalled directly (in auditory terms material was remembered not in sentences but in fragments); that it varied with reference to the degree in which the words were imaged in the quality of the individual voice; that the imagery of the voice in its true character sometimes appeared without the recall of any words.

Kuhlmann also found changes in recall according to the lapse of time between hearing the material and testing for recall, which he did after one, three and six weeks. The greatest changes occurred between the immediate and the second recall. There was a striking transformation from the immediate to the last recall, in both the manner of recall and the final result, in the auditory imagery of the words. Visual imagery was not constant in immedicate recall; it preceded the auditory in most cases in the last recall, and increased in amount, so that the visual imagery alone presented the whole scene and event. The general clearness and vivacity of the visual imagery remained about constant throughout the several recalls.

The total amount recalled in auditory terms decreased markedly, sometimes leaving only a sentence or two that could be recalled after six weeks' interval. The fragmentary character of the recall, however, did not increase much.

There were progressive stages in the quality of auditory imagery: first, the voice was imaged in its individual quality; next it was imaged merely as a bass or tenor; after that it appeared in a somewhat characterless fashion; and finally there was no definite or complete auditory imagery at all before the words were formulated and stated in the recall.

The processes involved in memorizing also changed. At first, attention was divided between actual sounds and visual imagery. The first repetition or two brought with them the process of naming sounds and imitating them. During further repetitions visual imagery and naming quickly disappeared, and motor processes of imitation increased for a while, but tended finally, to drop out.

Kuhlmann had his subjects recall sounds in a semi-passive way, without making any effort in the direction of detail or vividness. In 53% visual imagery appeared first, in 15% naming the subject of recall came first, and in 8% motor processes came first. Visual imagery preceded auditory imagery in 55%, the name preceded the auditory image in 24% and motor processes preceded auditory imagery in 13%.

Visual imagery was described as consisting of the things that produced the sounds (although attention to visual imagery for purposes of recalling details proved detrimental to recall); of the things going through the motions they would make in producing the sounds; or of visual sound analogues, consisting of arbitrary forms, sometimes including colors, whose characteristics were patterned after the characteristics of the sounds.

The motor processes which were used in imitating the sounds were inseparably connected with the effort to recall the sound vividly and minutely.

The auditory imagery was very fragmentary, and could not usually be directly controlled voluntarily, but only through motor processes, or in some instances, through visual imagery.

Sleep-learning observers have pointed out that some time periods are more favorable to learning and some less. Edward Van Ormer conducted an investigation to determine the best time for study in terms of how well we remember later what we have learned. He examined retention after intervals of sleep and waking and found that on the whole recall was most efficient after sleep. Other investigators he reported on came to the same general conclusion; Jenkins and Dallenback said that "forgetting is not so much a matter of the decay of old impressions and associations as it is a matter of interference, inhibition, or obliteration of the old by the new." Heine said improved memory resulting from "sleeping on" the learned material was due to the elimination of the retroactive inhibition produced by the day activities which normally follow learning.

Van Ormer goes along with this. He explains that sleeping after studying gives best results because of the absence of the inhibition or obliteration of the learned material by the waking activity. He theorizes that another factor enters into it, that it is possible that the waking activity not only inhibits and obliterates what has been learned, but that it also prevents or holds in check a preservation or consolidation process which continues for a while in the nervous system after the impression of the learned material. This preservation or consolidation process may often be at its highest point for the first part of the hour following learning. He suggests that it is also possible that the process of waking and the activity that takes place before there is any relearning is inhibitory as well. Still, he points out, results show there is a preservative process.

Van Ormer offers the explanation that perhaps recall is benefited by the refreshing effect of sleep on the organism, but notes that the same results were achieved whether the subject slept one hour or eight hours. Moreover, the results were the same one hour after the study period regardless of whether the hour was spent sleeping or waking.

The results suggested, on the whole, that a primary factor in forgetting is the action of the interpolated activity, because it inhibits a consolidation or preservation process and produces inhibition and obliteration of learned material. Retention was, for the most part, better after four or eight hours of sleep than after the same time interval of waking.

Little is forgotten during sleep. This appears to be an argument in favor of late night study, and perhaps also in favor of "cramming" before examinations.

A. E. Wagner conducted one of the early experiments "to determine the number of repetitions necessary to memorize and retain with maximum certainty a miscellaneous collection of facts." He noted the effectiveness of Jesuit methods of thorough and repeated drill and was thus inspired to study the value of frequent repetition. He concluded that it was best to employ a relatively small number of repetitions with a constantly increasing interval of time between the repetitions, continuing over a rather long time period. His results showed that high school students, on the average, needed six repetitions (of his selected miscellaneous facts), and grade school students averaged about seven repetitions.

The physiological explanation of memory generally accepted today is that everything we experience or learn produces some physical change in the brain, leaves some kind of a trace, sometimes called an engram.* Weinland suggests that the memory trace may be a lowering of the resistance to passage of the nervous impulse from one cell to another, so that the next impulse passes across more easily.

We have already discussed Thorndike's laws of learning, which state the importance of motivation, repetition, reward and meaningfulness; and the Gestalt emphasis on the whole, the meaningful configuration. (Weinland points out a danger of inaccuracy with regard to detail in the Gestalt principle.)

Weinland does not agree with the memory improvement authorities that anyone can be trained to have a good memory. Improvement is certainly possible, but the one invariable is the person's potential. This cannot be increased. He tells us that psychologists agree with William James that retentiveness, that is, capacity for remembering, cannot be improved by effort or training,

---

* The communication system between the cells of the nervous system is the physical basis of the association of ideas in the brain. Brain injury, lobotomy, or disease of the brain have been shown to affect certain areas of the brain, but not all.

because it is dependent on the brain structure. Within the limits of the potential, however, memory can be improved like any other skill.

Among the common and useful memory devices that many people employ without outside instruction are numbering, classifying, and visualizing. Those who have not learned to use these devices by themselves can gain in efficiency by applying themselves in this way. Motivation is important too—not just in the sense of wanting to improve one's memory—but in the more particular sense of wanting to learn specific things for specific purposes.

The more driving the need or desire, the more effective will be the memory.

Interest is important, and explains the fact that memories, even remarkable memories, are usually especially good in only one area. People with amazing memories for things in general are probably interested in everything. Weinland concludes that a person's memory can be called poor only if he forgets many things that deeply interest him after making an effort to remember them.

Sometimes forgetting is simply a matter of incomplete learning due to lack of attention or interest. An impression has never really been made on the mind. Weinland and others think there may be evidence that nothing experienced is ever completely forgotten, unless there is a brain injury or atrophy. The explanation that forgetting is the result of fading of the trace is contradicted by the recovery of many forgotten memories in the course of psychotherapy, by association, and also in hypnotherapy, where patients have been 'regressed' and, under hypnosis, even speak and write like a child of the age desired, with emotions and experiences to match, unchanged by what happened later in the subject's life.

It has also been found that recall of meaningful materials is as much as 50% better under hypnosis. Recall is also better in other states characterized by relaxation—abstraction, free association, "twilight sleep," and simple relaxation.

Brain injuries sometimes result in loss of memory, but not always. Often there is no noticeable amnesia, or it is temporary. The location in the brain of the injury (or of surgery) makes a difference in the effect on memory. Certain diseases may result in amnesia, for instance, syphilis, epilepsy and Korsakoff's disease (a result of alcoholism). A serious lack of oxygen or blockage of blood circulation through the brain can have permanent destructive effects on the brain and therefore on aspects of memory.

Deterioration of memory with the years may be part physiological, and part psychological, Weinland says. It is physiological when an old person forgets things he wants to remember, but it is psychological when he forgets things which have become unimportant to him. Both factors contribute to the apparent fine memory for events of childhood and youth and poor memory for recent events.

Weinland tells us that according to the evidence, brain damage is greater in its effect on memory of recent events, and in addition the present and future are frequently less important to old people who may find more satisfaction in remembering earlier happiness. Loss of interest in life makes them dismiss memories of no importance, then the ever present tendency to forget what we don't care about remembering takes over. But generalizations cannot be made; some old people remain mentally alert and suffer no serious memory loss, and they make up for such as there is by experience, accumulation of knowledge, ability to organize, and increased capacity to comprehend.

Weinland goes on to state that some forgetting is active, or defensive—selective, in order to clear the mind of material irrelevant to the immediate purpose. He reminds us that Pavlov found that associations can be unlearned.

Freud said we bar unpleasant things from consciousness, and sometimes complicate the forgetting—and betray ourselves—with what are known now as Freudian slips. He found that childhood experiences which had lasting and damaging effects but were apparently forgotten, had merely been repressed because they were too disturbing to be admitted, and that these incidents could be recalled with sufficient effort and encouragement.

Weinland reports that the theory that we forget unpleasant things has been tested, and that the findings indicate that usually pleasant things are remembered better than unpleasant things, but there is no great difference quantitatively. Further, both pleasant and unpleasant things are remembered better than indifferent things, and pessimists tend to remember unpleasant things and forget pleasant ones. Repression, then, exists in one way or another. Amnesia is a complete escape through repression; this frequently proves to be disturbing and thus a motivation is created for recovery. Small-scale amnesia, or "blacking out," is often protective. Repression can also operate for reasons of pride, to avoid anxiety and to make past memories more acceptable by alteration of the facts.

Memories fade more rapidly when they are not in use or reviewed. (Here Weinland makes a distinction between recall and recognition; the former is lost much more quickly than the latter.) But the material learned is not altogether lost, for it can be relearned in less time than was necessary when the material was completely new.

In the course of his experimentation, Ebbinghaus found that forgetting begins rapidly and then slows down. Davis and Moore tested retention and found that material meaningful to the learner was remembered better. Nadorah Smith reported that with material retained for a long time the forgetting process is slowed down considerably. E. J. Smith found retention high in motor acts; he explained this as due to the fact that greater organization is required for this sort of learning, and Weinland adds that since motor learning is often overlearning, retention is further aided.

The interference of emotional factors (e.g., love, fear, anger, insecurity) can cause forgetting, as can another manifestation of complete concentration—absent-mindedness.

Forgetting can sometimes be attributed to blocking of the item for which recall is desired.

And finally, when a task is completed, it is frequently forgotten because the mind has decided there is no further need to remember anything about it.

Proceeding from investigation of the nature of re-

112

membering and forgetting, various authorities have attempted to devise principles, rules, and systems to aid in improvement of memory. Somewhere around 500 B. C. Simonides worked out a system of assigning things to be remembered, a position in space, a method also employed by Quintilian and Cicero. In the seventeenth century Henry Hudson applied a similar system involving association by visual symbol. A complicated digit-letter system was used as far back as the fifteenth century, appeared in Germany in the seventeenth century, and in England in the nineteenth century; this approach involves considerable practice and is applicable only to rote learning. It is also useful for theatrical type stunts. Successive-comparism systems—broad associations in a kind of chain systems—have been invented; these often require remembering as much inventive associational material as can be found in the already logically associated material of a well-planned text. Another system was based on paired associations, like pen and ink, and combined number associations with visual imagery of absurd combinations which were presumed to make the combination, and thus the key word, memorable. Known as the Roth Memory Course, its major value is in the field of entertainment and for particular occasions, not for lengthy retention.

Weinland's principles behind memory improvement stress the importance of interest, of selection, of complete attention, of accuracy in the first learning against speed, of proper instruction if necessary, of understanding (meaningful learning), of background associations to reinforce the meaning and discrimination to discern relatedness, of the "mental set" or intention to remember

—effective even for a specific length of time—of confidence that we can remember, of a reasonable degree of ego involvement, of specific meaningful associations or connections, of a background of knowledge, of good organization and classification of the material ("A good memory is like a well organized and well maintained filing system," he writes), of combining whole and part learning, of dividing material to be learned into separate groups in order to simplify the task and of reinforcing the memory by repetition and use.

Weinland rephrases the above principles for remembering a particular fact:

1. Try to see its significance, try to be interested in it, or at least in the value of remembering it.
2. Give it your attention; be sure you have it right.
3. Be sure you fully understand it.
4. Intend to remember it.
5. Be confident you can remember it.
6. Involve the ego if possible.
7. Associate it with other related facts.
8. File it in its proper place in your memory system.
9. See it as a part of a larger whole.
10. If there is a basis for doing so, learn it as part of a small group of related facts.

In discussing study methods, Weinland emphasized the importance of an environment conducive to study. He too points out the value of using all the senses to reinforce memory, and reminds us that verbalization can be an aid to motor learning. In discussing the auditory and visual aspects, he refers to an investigation by F. C.

Bartlett, who found that visual memorizers tend to be quick and confident in their learning and in reproducing the subject matter—quite directly—with less dependency on grouping, comparisms and secondary associations than auditory memorizers, who in addition reached for signs and cues and descriptions, and who are less confident in recalling subject matter.

On the other hand visual memorizers were more likely to change the material in recall, or to change the order or add material not originally included. A combination of the two is, of course, preferable to either one method alone. Visual aids are always useful in fixing a memory, as are efficient reading habits. Marking up a book or taking notes in a lecture also help, by further affixing attention in the course of learning and for furture reference when review is necessary, as does recitation for the purpose of self-testing. Review soon after learning, because of the quick early forgetting tendency, is useful, and spaced practice is important. Weinland tells us that sometimes the review is more meaningful if there are slight changes in method or point of view; this is of interest in our study because the sleep-learning investigations report better results when the material is not changed.

The recommendations to study before going to sleep are modified by Weinland, "unless physically or mentally overtired." He also recommends, on the basis of several studies, learning the material in the evening before going to bed and reviewing it the next morning. He too values overlearning, but feels it should be used with discretion. And he notes that miscellaneous items can best be remembered by finding a pattern or principle for it: a pattern in the spelling or in the arrangement of numbers, in features and appearance and behavior of people, in the rhythm and melody of music, in the customs of a group, and in suffixes in language; a principle of spelling or grammar rules, a principle behind group customs which presents them in a unified way—and so forth.

Rhyme, numbering, alphabetical order, abbreviation, a kind of acrostic system of making words out of first letters of a series of facts, pigeonholing (Simonides' spatial arrangment), translation of numbers and letters already referred to, paired associates and chain associations (also referred to above) are all mentioned by Weinland as memory devices that have some value but also limitations. Numbering ceases to be useful when large numbers of items are to be considered; alphabetical order may result in blocking; abbreviation can be confusing, or even come before remembering the whole fact for which the abbreviation stands; acrostics are artificial and may discourage attempts to understand the material; pigeonholing is not a good substitute for arrangement by logic and organization; number letter translation is a complication requiring special learning and practice and appears to be useful for little more than tricks; paired associates and chain association have been discussed elsewhere and are not recommended for wide use. But all of these devices can be useful and helpful in particular circumstances.

Since reports on sleep-study point to so much success in learning foreign languages it will be interesting to consider what wide-awake learners have to say on the subject. Weinland considers interest and enthusiasm of primary importance, interest not only in the language, but in the country where it is spoken. Conversing with a person for whom this is the native tongue, and reading newspapers and magazines in the language serve both to heighten interest and practice. Pictures and advertisements help the beginner to understand the captions in foreign literature. Knowledge of current events through reading paper in English (or the student's own language) makes it easier to understand articles on the subject in a foreign paper. Subscribing to periodicals also offers good spaced practice, which is found useful in remembering. The card system, with the foreign word on one side and the English word on the other, is recommended, with frequent practice in self-testing. Attention and accurate first learnings, with awareness of both the similarity to and the difference from the English equivalent, are stressed. A combination of the visual and auditory aspects of both the word and the thing it represents is neessary to make the subject think in a new language. Finding the relatedness among various foreign words is valuable, and idioms too, must be tied together. Reciting and self-testing in writing is essential, especially for the grammar.

Surveying the recommendations of the memory experts, what conditions and methods do we find conducive to recall? And how far does sleep-learning coincide with these findings?

We find consistency in many areas. There is agreement that certain time periods are better than others, that study just before sleep helps avoid retroactive inhibition of memory, also that motivation, knowledge of achievement, reinforcement by review, thinking about the material, learning during spaced intervals, understanding and repeating are vital. Reciting and writing out the material, relaxation, interest, confidence, health and freedom from drugs, overlearning, reinforcement of motor learning with verbalization, the proper environment, and general conditioning or habit formation are also important and helpful elements of memory.

The effort to forget does not seem to be important in sleep-learning, since this form of memory stems directly from subconscious activity. If that constant evaluation of progress indicates worry, anxiety, and possible barriers in the early stages, it is implicitly considered undesirable in sleep-learning as in conscious memorizing. Meaningful material is easier to learn both awake and asleep, according to the authorities of both schools. Association and coexistence are not stressed, except as a general free-association activity in connection with repetition, in the literature of sleep-research, nor is there too much discussion of whole and part learning, broken and serial presentation, or grouping of material.

Sleep-study advocates report no age limitations in learning capacity in older people, and seem to disagree that there are individual limits to learning potential. But they all agree that incentive is important, and the entire system of sleep-learning precludes the possibility of wandering or divided attention. They recognize the interference of emotional problems and recommend sleep-therapy as a means of overcoming these. They seem not to be directly concerned with home influence and social training, although these are probably recognized as part of the emotional attitude. Distortion of interpretation is hardly likely during the first learning, since the subject is asleep, and the possibility of distortion occurring is subsequently not mentioned.

Accuracy of first learning seems to be assured, if the tape has been prepared correctly and accurately.

The question of whether the material is pleasant or unpleasant or indifferent and the effect on memory is not dealt with. Reports indicate that rote learning of just about anything is possible, but incentive and motivation and interest are recommended, so this can conceivably be related to the pleasure-displeasure theories.

Efficient techniques, selectivity and organization of material, finding underlying principles or patterns—all these are recommended by sleep-learning advocates as part of the learning process.

Consistent with psychologists' findings is that auditory learning, which is the basis for sleep-learning, has been found to be more effective than visual learning.

Among the conscious aids to memory which are helpful to a degree, few appear to be important in sleep-study. Numbering, classifying, visualizing, spatial arrangement, digit number systems, paired or chain associations, abbreviations—these are not mentioned at all. Rhyme is referred to as the easiest material to learn during sleep, and is thus recommended to begin with. Ego involvement is certainly apparent in the sleep-therapy recordings, as well as in the relaxing and preludes to sleep-learning tapes.

It would be inteersting if the sleep-learners were able to conduct tests to discover whether or not memory acquired during sleep suffers in recall from proactive inhibition (previously learned material) or from blocking, and what degree of cue dependency is involved in this method.

According to testimonials, students who learned foreign languages during sleep achieved amazing results in a short time. When we compare these claims with the busy schedule recommended by authorities on conscious learning of a language, we can only gasp at the time and effort saved. Again tests should be conducted to discover how well the student acquires the living feel of the language, understanding and accuracy in the use of grammar, and whether or not he thinks in the new language.

On the whole, there appears to be enough consistency in the theories of conscious memory and sleep-memory to indicate considerable validity in the latter approach.

Certain conscious effort must still be made, if the knowledge thus acquired is to be used intelligently. But the degree to which drilling and rote learning, which are required in many areas of study, can be shortened will obviously stimulate interest and incentive to experiment with the possibility of sleep-study.

chapter IX

Hypnosis and Sleep-Learning

Theodore X. Barber of the Department of Psychology of American University conducted tests in 1956 comparing suggestibility during sleep and hypnosis, and found his subjects as suggestible in one state as the other. Since many professionals equally endorse hypnotism and sleep-learning and sleep-therapy, the results of the experiment bear out even further the claims and theories upon which sleep-education is based. And since there is so much similarity between the two states, it follows that much or all of what can be accomplished by hypnosis may also be accomplished by sleep-learning and sleep-therapy.

Hypnotherapist Rita Sperling reports that the dual application of sleep-learning or sleep-therapy and direct hypnosis has provided her with the most nearly perfect tools of therapeutic treatment. Her controlled tests over the years have been extraordinarily successful.

In 1957, Pope Pius XII sanctioned the use of hypnosis as an anaesthetic.

A recent article on hypnosis in *Life* magazine, while noting that hypnosis is not, most certainly, a cure-all and will not bring recovery from illness except when used along with other medical treatment, describes its potential value in treatment of physical illness where there is a definite emotional element involved. Among the problems mentioned as responsive to help by hypnosis and hypnotherapy are asthma, anxieties, compulsions, phobias and harmful habits such as smoking, drug addiction and alcoholism. Hypnotism may also help strengthen a desire to live or bring peace of mind, according to this report. It can, by suggestions, set off conditioned reflexes and even affect physiological processes.

Apparently hypnotherapy will not work on everybody. Perhaps 15% of the population is resistant to it, for reasons of extreme youth (children under four) or senility, feeble mindedness, and various emotional or mental conditions. Of the rest, it is calculated that 85% can achieve the second stage, and about 40% the deep stage. Only about 20% can be somnambules. But since the trance depth can be increased by practice, perhaps those experts who say every normal person is a potential somnambule are right. No matter, since the very deep trances are not required for effective hypnosis. The benefits of hypnosis can be had while in the lightest stages, upon total acceptance of the suggestions offered. It is, however, interesting to note, that these figures are in constant change, always leaning toward a greater percentage than before who are liable to hypnotic suggestion.

Life reports that the most important aspect of hypnosis lies in the capacity to relieve stress and anxiety. There has been considerable success in the treatment of peptic ulcers, and also in the treatment of dyspepsia, chronic gastritis, colitis, high blood pressure, rapid pulse, heart palpitations, impotence and frigidity, poor bladder control, menstrual difficulties, and skin disorders such as eczema and hives. Babies have been delivered under hypnosis and bad habits like bed wetting and even blushing have been eliminated. Motivation is stressed as important, of course, and along with this hypnosis has been employed to break the smoking habit, to overcome insomnia, and to reduce and gain weight.

Weight reduction experiments reported by Dr. Lawrence B. Winklestein in the *New York State Journal of Medicine* were extremely successful. On the other end of the scale loss of appetite has been overcome.

A series of articles in the *New York Post,* May 1959 describes the successful personal hypnotic reducing experience of a female reporter of that paper.

Life reiterates the warning found in all responsible literature on the subject—that symptom removal must be used with caution; the cause of the disturbance should be treated lest another symptom replace the one being eliminated. Many hypnotists however claim that bad effects of symptom removal, where it is indicated, were at a minimum. Mrs. Sperling, director of the Professional Hypnosis Institute, indicates that she has found the ideal symptom substitution is the elimination of the detrimental symptom, and the resultant pride of the accomplishment.

The following is quoted from her notes on the combined uses of hynosis and sleep-learning: "In considering the role of hypnosis in correlation with the technique of sleep-learning, we must note that in some instances there appears the physchological block against sleep-learning.

"This was the experience of 'G'. 'G' contacted the Professional Hypnosis Institute because he had been advised to try hypnosis in getting through the barrier. During his interview 'G' explained that he had invested in the sleep-learning equipment—over his wife's objections. He followed the directions that arrived with the equipment but his results left much to be desired. To add to his irritation, his wife was getting results where he was not! The explanation to 'G'—"You are getting out of your efforts exactly in proportion to your subconscious expectations; and in the degree that your mental energies are being displaced in doubt of the workability of the sleep-learning program; if your mental energies are being depleted in emotional preoccupation with discouragement, disappointment, irritation, anxiety and such negative considerations, for whatever the reason or reasons, then you have only a limited portion of your total mental potential available for constructive application to the sleep-learning technique. You might just as well attempt to drive your car with both hands behind your back." When 'G' came into the course at PHI, approximately one-half hour was allotted to the combined uses of hypnosis and sleep-learning. Information was sparse at that time. However, since 'G's results and those of successive students, this phase of the instruction has been given considerable increase. Our knowledge, by actual student experience, has expanded to include the deliberate formation of character, personality and behavior traits, the learning of specific material and even weight reduction—all taught as an adjunct to the course instruction, during sleep.

"While 'G' was taking the course with PHI he was also attending a course in public speaking. He attended class on Monday night and went to PHI on Tuesday night. The results in the former were so influenced by the latter that he completed the public speaking course in top position, after so humble a beginning as to find it almost impossible to face the students and speak his own name. 'G's first experience with sleep-learning while attending PHI was so dramatic that it threw open the door which lead to all of his subsequent successes.

"It is important that we note that, despite the student's assumption that he should "feel" the absorption of the study material, there is, in fact, no clearly definable alteration beyond the understanding that learning has taken place and the information learned will spring into action in the appropriate circumstances, as in the case of a test or exam. In the common study methods, the conscious mind is deeply involved and so there is a conscious awareness of having learned.

"It was decided to offer 'G' definite proof that he had successfully absorbed the study material. This was done through the simple expedient of placing 'G' under hypnosis and advising him that, post-hypnotically, he would, during class at PHI, write his previously recorded study material in his notebook. This "proof of acceptance" was all that was required. 'G' then continued on to continued sucesses with sleep-learning.

"Student 'M' became a sleep-learner to further her attempts with weight reduction. Her husband took a dim view of the sleep-learning method, considerably dampening 'M's enthusiasm. 'M' had many times before spoken of her husband's tensions which caused somewhat strained relations in their family which included five youngsters. A demanding domination seemed to be the keynote of his personality. As an experiment, PHI suggested the temporary abandonment of the reducing program in favor of a tape couched in terms of general wellbeing, using the third person format, i.e., "You are a calmer and happier person. You feel a sense of confidence and contentment, etc." Convincing her husband that this approach would make her a happier and more effective wife and mother, 'M' secured her husband's reluctant approval to use the sleep-learning equipment. As planned, she arranged the pillow speaker so that he too could hear the material while he slept.

"Before a week had passed, 'M's husband was undergoing a change. He was more patient with her and the children; he was more ambitious with regard to business; he was less demanding and more lenient; his general outlook was noticeably improved; he appeared happier in general. This was nothing short of a miracle to the student ('M'). It is interesting to note that 'M's husband was not aware of these changes. To date, 'M' is not aware if her husband had knowledge of the use of the technique; he has not made any mention of it. She has since used sleep-learning to further her own goals, shedding forty-four pounds in approximately four months. She is now using her sleep-learning knowledge to study for her real estate and insurance examination for brokerage, joining her husband in the field.

"Student 'T' came to PHI near the end of his high

school term. He wanted to use sleep-study to study for his final exams. Within five days of this decision he was to take four exams and didn't know how or with which subject to begin. A sleep-study script was prepared for 'T' designed to refresh his memory on each of the subjects, taking into consideration all of his school experience. It was suggested that whatever he had seen, heard, read or practiced with respect to each of his subjects, all of this information would be available to him and support him in the taking of each exam. 'T' was elated with the results. His marks outdistanced all of his previous experience with final exams.

"Another student 'T' came to PHI after having failed a subject in high school, receiving a conditional graduation. It was now July and he was in the process of some accelerated study on the failed subject. At this point he was anything but optimistic and this was his reason for seeking help. A month did not afford much time, but using the techniques, 'T' again took the exam and came up with a mark of 100%.

"Student 'R' had a very violent temper, which delivered him into all types of difficulty, especially with his young wife. It was arranged that he and his wife understand the difficulties beyond the temper problem. 'R' began to use sleep-learning to change his entire approach to life. His work consumes a great deal of his time; however, sleep-learning allows him the additional time for study that he requires.

"Student 'W' is 14 years old. His father, an alumnus of PHI, brought him for training. For most of his young life, 'W' suffered what was considered a thyroid condition, producing a problem of overweight. Too, his dad wanted to have a better understanding of his abilities and his potential. Up to this time 'W' had been on a rather strict diet and there had been some weight loss over the years. After completion of the course at PHI, his father obtained sleep-learning equipment for him. Within one week, 'W's subconscious accepted a new self-image—slim, and healthy. The young man lost his excess weight so easily that his father felt the need to slow the process. He reworked the sleep-study script to have the boy's weight maintain the norm for his age and height, and to remain consistent with his growth.

"Student 'L' was telling about her two-year old son, 'J'. 'J' loved to torment the house kitten and invariably ended up crying in pain and resentment when the kitten clawed the child in self-defense. This was a frustrating situation for all concerned. One night, after 'J' was sleep, 'L' purred some soft suggestions into his ears. He hasn't bothered the cat since."

Conclusions reached concerning the associative value of sleep-learning with hypnosis are obvious. It is important to note that prior to use of any study technique, the student should have complete awareness of the subject. The combination of understanding and the repetitive conditioning technique of sleep-learning then lead to progressive results in any area.

In many instances, as reported by *Life*, hypnosis has been used along with deep therapy with success, sometimes to remove resistances and leave the patient accessible to psychotherapeutic help.

In the June, 1960, article in *Pageant* magazine by Gerald Walker, it is stated that hypnosis has become a powerful medical tool. Dr. Milton V. Kline, Research

Project Director for Hypnosis at Long Island University, states that the usefulness and value of hypnosis "are as infinite as the capacities of the human mind, of which it is a function." The *Pageant* article goes on to state that the cautious American Medical Association officially pronounced hypnosis "a useful technique in the treatment of certain illnesses." The AMA held a symposium on the use of hypnosis in major surgery and more research and better instruction in all its therapeutic uses.

The *Pageant* article also mentioned that an estimated 5,000 U.S. physicians use hypnosis. Dentists, psychiatrists, psychoanalysts and clinical psychologists are taking advantage of the benefits of using hypnosis in treatment.

In 1958 the AMA Mental Health Council's report on hypnosis urged that the science of suggestion should be taught in medical schools.

In England hypnosis has been utilized as a medical and therapeutic aid since its enthusiastic endorsement by the British Medical Assoication in 1955.

There are sometimes short-lived uncomfortable posthypnotic symptoms, but hypnosis in itself is harmless, according to *Life*. It is agreed that subjects will do nothing during hypnosis that is in contradiction to their own values or that threatens their self-preservation. On the other hand, strong criminal tendencies, otherwise latent, may be released. Because we are all a mixture of social and anti-social impulses, it is stressed again that in hypnosis the integrity and competence of the practitioner are of great importance.

Dr. Frank A. Pattie of the University of Kentucky helped people to wear contact lenses through hypnosis. It is believed that, if applied to education, hypnosis may be able to increase comprehension, retention, speed of learning and general efficiency, and also supply motivation to learn, and to achieve pleasure in performance. A violinist improved her technical performance without playing or looking at music, simply hallucinating a practice session in distorted time. (Hypnosis has been able to create the illusion of time flying or standing still.)

At this time, sleep-learning can achieve results to rival those of hypnosis, and, most important, since the technique does not require an experienced practitioner (the most successful results are achieved when the sleep-learner records his own material) it benefits directly the person involved. The mechanical and electronic tools of sleep-learning are easily used by the learner, since he himself is in the position to determine the suggstions placed during sleep-study.

Sleep-learning techniques have improved memory, trained children, speeded up learning, taught languages with correct pronunciation, raised school marks, increased music appreciation, eliminated bad habits and emotional blocks, rendered a minimum of sleep sufficient, upped salespeoples' capacities, eliminated nightmares and insomnia, and aided in relaxation and positive outlook.

It is most essential that we recognize hypnotism stripped of the false raiment in which it has been clothed by history. The hypnotist is not a super-endowed being; with applied study and training, we are all hypnotists.

Since the door to the subconscious is best opened by suggestion, there is an evident relationship between hypnosis and sleep-learning.

chapter X

Pro and Con

We have progressed.

Not too many decades ago, in times that were then considered enlightened, we burned people at the stake for original thoughts or conceptions. Dr. Ignatz Semmelweiss was nearly ostracized from the medical profession because he advocated the simple cleansing of hands when leaving the dissection room. In Dr. Semmelweiss' times, there existed a great incidence of death during childbirth. His logical assumption, that the disease harbored in the cadavers of the dissecting room could be carried by the doctors to the maternity wards, was openly ridiculed for many years, in spite of the ample proof presented over these years by Dr. Semmelweiss. This was, after all, a simple request, the washing of one's hands. Fortunately, Dr. Semmelweiss did finally triumph over the negative persistency of his contemporaries.

Hypnosis has suffered for many years because of the misstatements which were accepted as established fact. The "evil eye" of Svengali, who influenced Trilby in all the tradition of the mystics, did a great deal to curtail the rapid advance of what is today accepted as a logical progression of the human ability. Today hypnotism has had much of the cloak of mystery surrounding it removed by responsible people, and now that the subject is more completely understood, is in constant use medically and therapeutically. The American Medical Association has recognized its value, and the American Dental Association offers information for use of the technique.

Sleep-learning is no stranger to these negative reactions. But, since the use of the technique continues to grow, with established proofs and verifications constantly available, it is daily gaining more recognition and acceptance by the recognized "authorities." There have been a great many tests to determine the actual value of the technique. Studies that inquire into the reason for individual receptivity of the student have given us many answers. Some studies have proved positive, some negative, and some hang in the middle.

There have been very few official studies of sleep-learning. The research is being done, for the most part, by the proponents of the technique that are sincerely anxious for all information on the subject. There have been a few controlled studies, which are mentioned in this book. For the most part, the information gleaned is from individuals who have used this system of learning, either successfully or unsuccessfully. The successful projects are noted, of course, but the failures in the use of the technique are more thoroughly examined. It is from the student's ability or inability to accept the recorded message that the sleep-learning researchers learn most. In most cases it has been learned the negative thoughts by the attempting sleep-student caused the greatest percentage of failures. Sleep-learning researchers stress the importance of positive assertions for successful learning, either awake or asleep. In some cases, no determination has been made as to the reasons for failure. It is suspected that the same condition holds in learning awake or asleep: there are many poor students to whom the basic need is motivation and concentration.

It has never been suggested that sleep-learning is the "cure-all" for negative thinkers or learners who will extend no effort to the learning process. It has been established, however, that sleep-learning is an extremely useful adjunct to the accepted learning techniques. After all, in sensible consideration, the technique of sleep-study enables one to take advantage of the third of life that is normally "lost." There can be little argument with the use of this available time, since it doesn't disturb rest; indeed, in most cases, it renders the learning process "painless," taking advantage, as it does of the unique abilities of the subconscious to accept, retain, sort and project learned material. Extensive studies of the learning process are actively continued, and with each new learned fact, the ability of the subconscious is stressed. This of course, further substantiates the benefits and advantages of learning while asleep.

Controlled studies are exceedingly important in research. It is these controls that enable the experts to evaluate the potential uses of any given experiment or technique. Of course, pre-judgment destroys the value of a research study. It is obvious that a negative assumption prior to testing will tend toward a negative conclusion.

Tests or controlled studies in sleep-learning are rare. Charles W. Simon and William H. Emmons effected a study of sleep-learning which started in April, 1955, continuing until October of that year. The Rand report, produced by Simon and Emmons, though considerable in size, and voluminous in text, seemed to be, as evidenced by the testing procedures followed, a superficial undertaking.

Initially, Simon and Emmons admit their lack of understanding of the physiological and psychological involvements of the sleep period. The determination of the various "stages" of sleep are still in a highly theoretical position. Simon and Emmons do admit that suggestion is accepted during "deep drowsiness," without defining the term.

The studies were carried out with 21 subjects of average intelligence. The subjects had, at all times, electroencyphenograph electrodes attached to determine the visual activity of alpha waves before sleep, during the various periods or stages of sleep, and during the sleep-learning periods.

Experiments lasted only for one night. The basic requirements of any form of successful learning, repetition, motivation, confidential approach, were completely ignored. And, with all of these unnatural conditions, the September 13, 1954 report indicates that ten studies did indicate some acceptance of learning while asleep. These noted ten studies were favorable under what we know now to be unfavorable sleep-learning conditions.

The Simon and Emmons report stresses that, in the instance where learning did take place during sleep, they were unable to determine if the subject was asleep. This, of course, returns to the inadequate definition of sleep that science is faced with.

The October 12, 1955 study of nine students with the EEG electrodes offered greater repetition, but other material was interspersed with the original study material. This is, of course, also highly unfavorable, since we are now well aware that concentration upon one subject material is important for sleep-study. The October 10th study admits success during the so-called "drowsy" state; again, an inadequate definition of sleep.

The conclusions to be reached from this testing by Simon and Emmons for the Rand Corporation are clear. The test processes of twenty-one students were based on only forty-eight repetitions of the material; these students underwent simultaneous EEG tests with attached electrodes. This, of course, would obviously induce anxiety and nervousness in the subjects, and could easily have instilled the psychological block we are now familiar with. With all this inadequacy, we find that the subjects did enjoy substantial learning success. The Rand report, however, stipulates that this learning did not take place during sleep. This premise, of course, established again without an adequate definition of sleep.

Today, on the other hand, we do find constant testing under modern, progressive conditions. One such test was conducted under the auspices of the Northside Center for Child Development, in New York City. Cecelia Pollack was the therapist in charge of this experiment for the Northside Center. Her report, "The Effect of Sleep

Learning in a Remedial Reading Situation" is being published in an international scientific journal. We have her permission to quote from this report.

"Statement of the problem:

In the course of teaching a brain-injured boy with serious reading problems how to read, there seemed to be a very basic problem. A normal amount of reinforcement in training to recognize sounds and synthesizing these sounds into words was totally inadequate. If there were years in which to provide this reinforcement, a phonic word attach could be taught, but Victor (the subject) was already seventeen years of age and about to learn a trade. The method of sight recognition had been tried and found almost useless because of the boy's poor visual and auditory memory."

Mrs. Pollack continues in this report with further definition of the subject and the testing technique. The subject, after his fourth trial with the control list of words, learned 13 words out of twenty well enough to blend them on the first attempt. He was still unable to blend seven words.

"On the other hand," Mrs. Pollack continues, "he was able to blend, on the first attempt after sleep-learning, 18 out of 20 of the experimental list and retained this high score at the second session. He was able to blend *all* the words at both the third and fourth sessions."

The report concludes with the consideration that, on the results of this study, it is possible to conclude that sleep-learning can hasten the process of learning to blend sounds into words. Mrs. Pollack's study has established conclusively that there is sufficient validity in the results to further explore the benefits of the technique in a remedial reading situation.

What can we conclude from this? That, with testing under intelligent, inquiring conditions and attitudes, we may well tap the brain for the advancement of the individual through sleep-learning.

We have consistently stated that no learning process yet achieved has reached the ultimate in teaching potential to the individual mind. Too, it must be remembered that honest appraisal of the technique will lead to more definitive conclusions that will eventualize in a more complete understanding of the learning process.

The proponents and the practitioners of the technique of sleep-study are anxious for independent research studies of sleep-learning.

There is no longer any question as to the validity of the technique in many areas. Its uses have been established in both emotional and educational areas. We can further advance the technique with these questioning studies and attitudes.

chapter XI

Modern Sleep-Learning

There have been substantial scientific advances since the early days of sleep-learning. Modern mechanical and electronic equipment has overcome the mechanical problems of sleep-study. We are now able to repeat the message to be learned endlessly with the aid of tape recorder and an endless tape device.

In 1929, Max Sherover, one of the pioneers in the mechanics of sleep-learning, wrote a science fiction story called "Cerebrophone, Inc." Here was an apparently fanciful excursion into the realm of sleep-education. Later, Sherover and a San Francisco engineer, Elmer Brown, produced the first sleep-learning device, using a combination of record player, electric clock, and under-the-pillow-speaker. They foresaw use of their invention in the fields of language teaching, treatment of emotional upsets, overcoming speech defects, and (as did Aldous Huxley) principle indoctrination.

In the early 1940's L. Leshan reported in the *Journal of Abnormal Psychology* that he found in his tests with this method that 40% of a group of fingernail biters became convinced by the message in the night that their fingernails tasted bitter, and gave up the habit, after being exposed to the message six times a night for fifty-four nights. In the same experiment a control group kept right on biting.

In the original testing of Sherover's machine, Charles R. Elliot of the University of North Carolina used fifteen unrelated three letter words on his sleeping subjects: boy, egg, say, art, run, not, sir, leg, bag, row, ice, out, age, box and eat. He verified that his subjects were asleep by the use of an electroencephalograph (Brain waves are different during sleep and wakefulness). The next day, this group, and a control group who had not heard the words in their sleep were asked to memorize the list of words. The first group learned the list 83% faster than the group which had not heard the words in their sleep. Elliot said he thought sleep-teaching was similar to re-teaching something the person has temporarily forgotten. In many instances this compulsion has been borne out. The familiarity with the material gained by sleep-study hastens conscious study.

Sherover reported that his students were learning languages 25% to 30% faster than students normally learn while awake.

In 1948, Sherover phophesied that the device could be used to teach such necessary information as multiplication tables, chemical formulas, the Morse code (Mr. Hugo Gernsback, as previously noted, points to the article by Chief Radioman J. N. Phinney, U. S. Navy, in which it is established that the technique was put into active practice for the study of Morse code in 1922; this article was published in *Radio News* magazine for October, 1923).

It was in 1949 that Chilean tenor Ramon Vinay's feat in sleep-learning a complete opera in accentless Italian became celebrated in music circles.

A 1952 newspaper report (*New York Times,* July 6th) informs us that the Morse code was taught to sleeping cadets.

In 1952 the *Journal of Experimental Psychology* reported tests which had been conducted at George Washington University: students were taught Chinese during sleep, between two-thirty and three A.M. The students were divided into three groups: the first group heard the Chinese words, but with mis-matched English words; the second group heard the Chinese words and their English equivalents; the third group heard Strauss waltzes. The first group required 11.1 repetitions; the second group mastered them in only 5.6 repetitions; and the third group needed 17.7 repetitions (so far as we know this group was not tested on their knowledge of Strauss waltzes).

An interesting side effect was the report of a girl who dreamed she was on a street in China; this was assumed to the influence of the Chinese words she heard in her sleep. This cannot be proved; the dream could have been caused by other associations, but it does invite speculations as to the degree of unconscious visual reinforcement present in sleep-learning. In any case, it is obvious that this student was highly susceptible to suggestion.

Bruno Furst, memory expert, stated that good memory is based on concentration and association, grouping of similar facts together, and then linking them by easy to remember mental pictures.

The last point—easy to remember mental pictures raises the question: could dreams be supplying this aspect of remembering for the material heard during sleep? Sleep-learning advocates explain that sleep-tapes achieve involuntary duplication or repetition of a desired specific mental picture, with a cumulative and powerful effect.

Tape machines are preferred to record players. The magnetic equipment of today allows the student to record and play back his study material immediately on the same instrument. Tape allows the absolute minimum of undesirable noise. A record can become worn and scratchy; the tape has an unlimited noise-free life. Any material available on records is easily transferrable to tape, and since tape operates on a principle of organization and reorganization of magnetic particles on the tape ribbon, when there is no further need for the study material presently recorded, tape can be easily erased by recording over the original material.

In addition, the material recorded on the tape by the student is much more effective, containing the combination of personal motivation and familiar voice and language that could not possibly be available on mass produced recordings. There are some pre-recorded tapes available, but the fault that is inherent with the pre-recorded records is carried over to this newer recording medium; it is logical to assume that the basics of successful personal sleep-study technique could not be available on pre-recorded material of any medium. We should also consider the elimination of duplicate expense when the student records his own material, and upon assimilating this study work, erases the tape as he records the new study material.

Any tape machine will operate well for sleep-study. It is not necessary to have "special equipment." Some sleep-learning organizations have combined the various components into an integrated group that is sold as a unit. The advantage here is that the various components have been matched to give good reproduction. Since tape recorders are available in a great many price ranges, your personal decision and needs will determine the limit of expense.

The next fundamental for sleep-study is the endless tape cartridge that will operate on any standard tape machine. This unique device will allow the material which is recorded by the sleep-student to be endlessly repeated while the recorder is on. The tape in this cartridge is automatically erased by the recorder as new material is recorded on it. These self-recorded messages are heard through a pillow speaker which is placed under the pillow, and, by controlling the volume on the tape recorder playback, will repeat the message for you alone. There are two types of pillow speakers presently available: the dynamic speaker, which is in reality a miniature speaker that is encased in a perforated metal container; this will allow the clearest reproduction. For those who are slightly hard of hearing, a speaker of the bone-conduction type is advertised, which operates as an under-the-pillow-speaker, but sets up audible vibrations through dense material, directly to the inner ear.

The automatic electric timer that can be set for the two nightly sleep-study periods is essential to sleep-learning. Without it, modern sleep-learning would be impossible, for the student would be required to be awake to switch the mechanism on and off. The timer simply connects to the wall outlet; the tape machine is connected to the receptacle in the timer. The timer is in effect, a clock that covers the twenty-four-hour cycle, automatically turning the recorder on and off the sleep-study periods, two and one-half hours after initially falling asleep, and for the one and one-half hour before awakening.

Beginners in the handling of tape recorders are cautioned to develop their microphone technique. The correct recording level must be determined before making the voice recording. This, however, is merely a matter of practice, and is easily mastered.

A distinct advantage of using tape is the lack of added expense for errors. Any errors in recording are immediately rectified by recording over the existing material. Endless tape cartridges, using the mobius loop with tape that is coated both sides, allows extended study material to be applied to the tape.

It is also worth mentioning that the tape recorder should have a connection whereby the speaker in the machine will be shut off when the pillow speaker is put into use.

Relaxation affirmations can either be recorded on a separate tape, or on the same tape as the study material. After some use of the technique, when the student is aware of his psychological acceptance of the recorded messages, it will not be necessary to use the relaxation affirmations; the information itself will beat a direct path to the subconscious.

The sleep-learner makes his own therapy tapes. When he does, he is advised to keep his sentences short and to the point, positive and optimistic; to use strong action verbs, avoiding too many adjectives and terminology that would be difficult to understand, or medical or scientific jargon that has no meaning for him. He must believe in himself and his message, must accept the idea and transform the idea into reality, both of which effects are achieved by the subconscious. A strong, commanding voice, calm and unhesitant, a voice that does not falter but reflects confidence and "dynamic certainty" is best. He should be sure of the proper microphone level in order that there be no distracting distortion in the recorded message, and use an automatic repeating tape device for repetition of the material.

There seems to be no limit to the capacity to learn. With the aid of modern study techniques, we can look forward to unlimited, beneficial learning. It is best to understand that we all have this capacity to learn, and the limits are set by us alone.

Your basic personality can be expanded through the use of affirmations on the sleep-tape of positive thinking: friendship, hope, forgiveness, peace, poise and will power. You can sharpen your bridge game, develop motor skills (all motor actions are originated in the mind; clarification of these motor skills accelerate your learning them). Secretaries can sharpen their shorthand and typing skills; learning a foreign language with sleep-study techniques now make the accumulation of many languages well within your grasp.

Your children can be presently prepared for their future by positive affirmations that will eliminate the need for future repairing of unwanted habits and actions. They can be led to self-confidence, magnetic personality, memory power, as well as instilling such good habits as an interest in learning, obedience to elders, sharing and unselfishness, cleanliness, neatness and good manners, along with eliminating such bad habits as bed wetting, nail biting, poor eating, stealing and cheating and lying. Fears and bad dreams can be overcome— and all while the child is asleep. Of course, the accomplishment of all these things could also eliminate the need of parents using the technique of sleep-learning to induce relaxation, bright philosophies, physical vitality, and a positive outlook on life.

' The "talking books" available on records can be transferred to the endless tape device for memorizing segments of a novel. It seems that the endless mechanism would not be a desirable adjunct to reading a novel. But perhaps, somewhere, sometime, there will be a sleep-student who must memorize a complete novel. After all who would have thought of sleep-teaching a parakeet?

chapter XII

Great Expectations

What may a newcomer to sleep-learning expect? Let us follow the procedure through completely:

Initially, the equipment required: a tape recorder that is capable of accepting a minimum of a five-inch reel of standard tape. This machine should operate by electricity, battery-operated sets are not suggested. In addition, the recorder must have a speaker output jack that will automatically disconnect the speaker in the recorder when the pillow speaker is inserted; a timing device that will operate to turn the tape machine on and off for the two sleep-study periods nightly; this will require a timer with a minimum of four trippers; an endless cartridge device that will allow the message that will be recorded thereon to be repeated endlessly; and last, an under-the-pillow-speaker that will bring the message directly to you from the tape machine. This should be of the dynamic type for the best fidelity.

It is advisable that you become familiar with the mechanical operation of the equipment. Operate the recorder using the standard reel-to-reel operation. Use the microphone to determine your best recording voice. In some instances you will detect sibilance, the hissing sound that will be recorded on the tape. Talking into the back of the microphone will usually eliminate this. Develop your microphone technique.

Inspect the endless cartridge device. The tape is pulled from the center of the cartridge through the tape head enclosure, and then returns to the side of the cartridge. The action of the tape in the cartridge is dependent on the recorder only at the place under the tape head cover where the capstan and pressure roller meet to pull the tape from the center of the cartridge; it automatically rewinds into the side of the cartridge. Though the cartridge is placed on the supply spindle of your recorder, this is but a positioning place, and the cartridge does not depend on the action of the supply spindle for operation.

After you have become familiar with the various mechanical components you have obtained for your sleep-studies, you will now want to start your sleep-learning work. And work it is. If you are anxious for a "miracle pill" to absorb this study material, neither sleep-learning nor, for that matter any known form of learning is your answer. The benefits of sleep-education are entirely dependent upon you. Your results will be in direct proportion to your effort.

For the novice in the use of sleep-study, it is advisable to start slowly. It is important to ascertain your understanding and acceptance of this form of study. Start with a short message that has some particular meaning for you when it will be learned. A poem or a group of phrases with rhythmic alliteration will be absorbed most easily.

Record this short message, about five or six minutes of material, on your endless cartridge. Take special care that you speak clearly and naturally into the microphone. The message you record will be the one you will hear over and over during the sleep-study periods, and it is important that it be clear and understandable.

The next step will be preparing the mechanical components for repetition of the material you have recorded. Insert the line cord of the tape machine into the outlet on the timer; connect the line cord of the timer to the wall outlet. Set the timer to your sleep-study periods on at your normal sleep-time, off two and one-half hours later—on again approximately one and one-half hours before you awaken, off as you awaken.

The endless cartridge device should then be placed on the supply reel of your tape recorder. The recorder is to be put in the play position, and the pillow speaker inserted. By rotating the clock face of the timer, you can now determine the action of the equipment. When the trippers on the timer turn the recorder on, the cartridge will start its action, and the message recorded on the tape in the cartridge will come through your pillow speaker.

Place the pillow speaker under your pillow (or, if you do not use a pillow, place it on the sheet near your head). Adjust the sound level from your tape recorder so that the message is just heard. As you drift off into sleep, the outside noises will fade out, and the minimum volume will be more than adequate.

Now, go to sleep. Try to erase the excitement that is normal in the start of a new endeavor from your mind.

Relax and allow the mechanical equipment to take over. Relaxation is a prime need for the sleep-student novice. You will find that you will drift slowly to sleep with the awareness of the repeating message. Welcome this message; you have recorded it, and it is material you want to learn.

How will you know you have absorbed the recorded material? It will affirm itself in your conscious mind in many ways; in some instances you will find that it will remain as learned material until you need the information, at which time it will automatically project itself to your conscious mind. The learned message may also appear immediately within a short time after the study time even if you have no need for the information. Many students find that the material sleep-learned projects itself as previously studied material, much like going over old study work.

It is important to understand that you will learn what you sincerely want to learn. And, understandably, successful sleep-learning will lead to more successful sleep-learning.

As you progress with the technique, you will find your own pattern of learning. Some material will require much shorter study period than others, as in conscious learning. You will find that you may want to intersperse study material with relaxation affirmations.

Learning takes place much more quickly and effectively when you are relaxed. This is true of any form of learning, conscious or subconscious. Sleep-learning assists you in reaching this state of relaxation preparatory to study.

Whether the technique is used for personality help

or development, or for standard study material, the requirements are the same: motivation or need to learn the material and understanding of the material to be learned. It is never advisable to combine two study subjects on the tape for the same study period. However, you can, if necessary, preface your study material with relaxation and tension elimination suggestions on your tape. These affirmations need not be lengthy; instead, they should be simple and to the point, explaining that you are now in a relaxed state, and welcome wholeheartedly the material which you have recorded.

The "script" used for sleep-study is of importance. Never use phrases or words you do not normally use in everyday activity. Couch the phrases so that the information is precise and to the point, with no flowery, extraneous wording or phrasing. Speak with confidence; remember, the message you record is the message you will hear. Confidence in your speaking voice will go a long way toward speedy assimilation of the material you want to learn. We refer you to the S.D.R.F. studies earlier in this book.

When studying rote material, it is only necessary to read the material onto the tape and allow the repetitious action of the cartridge during sleep-study periods accelerate reception.

Above all, remember that you are the absolute control over the material you want to learn, the personality development you are anxious to build. What you put into this study technique in the way of self-confidence and effort will repay itself to you many times over. You are the only and best judge of what and why you want to learn.

As you expand your knowledge and uses of the technique of sleep-learning you will find that you will have developed a new and greater appreciation of your present abilities and your future potential.

Remember always, you have unlimited capacities, only waiting for you to develop them to their fullest.

chapter XIII

The Ultimate Aid to Learning

Some of the literature referred to in our study of sleep-learning suggests that there is very little that cannot be learned, accomplished or cured by this method. The independent thinker will raise a skeptical eyebrow.

On the other hand, careful study of the evidence of responsible observers indicates that there is a great validity in the claims about sleep-learning. It can be, a valuable aid to, but not a substitute for, learning with the conscious mind.

In a study such as this, it is always preferable that we go as deep below the surface as possible. What have we found?

We do find minor contradictions, but that is to be expected in any technique as obviously progressive as this. It is constantly evident, however, that if the basic principles of sleep-learning were to be taken advantage of, without the extraneous matter which can attach itself to a new, powerful technique, we would all benefit. Simply taken, sleep-learning is not a talent restricted to the "chosen few." Indeed, the technique takes advantage of the basic abilities prevalent in everyone. There can be little doubt, when we consider the rapid advances of the past fifty years, that man seems to have unlimited capacities. Every day brings forth a new, exciting fact about our potential. When we look upon the technique of sleep-learning logically, we find that the evidence and the possibilities are most certainly available. It remains that we could, and should, take full advantage of them.

There has been a great and steady growth in the use of sleep-education in the past years, and it will continue to grow. Some large industrial corporations are investigating and using this form of training for their technical and sales personnel. An increasing number of therapists are supplementing their work with sleep-learning, to take full advantage of the reinforcement principles of their work. Students and instructors are supplementing their studies with sleep-learning.

Responsible advocates stress the importance of conscious understanding of the material, of intelligent organization and analysis, of review during waking hours, of motivation and of interest in the material to be learned.

Where it is necessary to learn lists or material not in itself meaningful, literally by rote, sleep-learning appears an absolute blessing. Most of our basic learning is rote material, necessary before we can go on to analytical thinking. If children can learn multiplication tables and the alphabet much more quickly and easily with this method, there seems to be little reason to quarrel with the idea, on the basis of knowledge available to us today. And if adults stock up on facts necessary in their fields painlessly, it is all to the good. It is to be hoped that mere accumulation of facts is not going to be substituted for understanding, evaluation, interpretation or analysis of material. There is a general tendency in our time to value information per se more highly than the ability to think.

Sleep-learning can aid greatly in time-saving, in increased efficiency, and in improving general knowledge. It will be up to the individual sleep-students to use it wisely.

Warnings that sleep-therapy should not be employed as a substitute for medical or psychotherapeutic treatment are evident in the literature of the responsible sleep-learning advocates. Again it is up to the individual to use the technique intelligently. But it is also the responsibility of the manufacturers and distributors of sleep-study equipment to make no extravagant claims, and, to caution the users toward intelligent use of the equipment. Used with understanding, sleep-learning can be of significant help in both the accumulation of study-material, and in personality development.

Sleep-learning's potential is staggering.

The beneficial uses of sleep-study have only just begun. It is indeed gratifying to see that this important scientific achievement is already claiming its rightful place among educational and learning techniques.

Bibliography

Bartley, S. H. Principles of Perception. New York: Harper & Bros. 1957.

Bechterev. V. M. General Principles of Human Reflexology. International Publishers, N.,

Dollard, John, and Miller, Neal E. Personality and Psychotherapy. New York: McGraw-Hill Book Co. 1950.

Dunlap, Knight. Habits, Their Making and Unmaking. New York: Liveright. 1932.

Elliot, Frank R. "Memory for Visual, Auditory and Visual-Auditory Material," Archives of Psychology, No. 199. New York, May, 1936.

The Basic Writings of Sigmund Freud. Translated and edited by Dr. A. A. Brill. New York: Modern Library. 1938.

Gernsback. Hugo. Modern Electrics, June 1911; Science and Invention, Dec., 1921; Radio News, October, 1923.

Guthrie, E. R. The Psychology of Learning. New York: Harper & Bros. 1952.

Hilgard, E. R. Theories of Learning. New York: Appleton-Century-Crofts. 1956.

Hollander, Bernard, M.D. Methods and Uses of Hypnosis and Self-Hypnosis. Hollywood, Cal.: Wilshire Book Co. 1957.

Hull, C. L. Principles of Behavior. New York: Appleton-Century-Crofts. 1943.

Hunter, Ian M. L. Memory, Facts and Fallacies, Baltimore: Penguin Books. 1957.

Jung, C. G. Two Essays on Analytical Psychology. New York: Meridian Books. 1956.

Kuhlmann F. "On the Analysis of Auditory Memory Consciousness" The American Journal of Psychology, Worcester, Mass. Vol. XX, 1909.

Life, March 7, 1960. "Hypnosis."

Powers, Melvin. Hypnotism Revealed. Hollywood, Cal.: Wilshire Book Co. 1952.

Professional Hypnosis Institute. Jersey City, New Jersey.

Research Bulletins. Self Development Research Foundation. 207 E. 37th St., New York.

Skinner, C. E. Essentials of Educational Psychology. Englewood Cliffs, N. J.: Prentice-Hall. 1958.

Thorndike, E. L. Human Learning. New York: Century. 1931.

Thorpe, Louis P., and Schmuller, Allen M. Contemporary Theories of Learning. New York: The Ronald Press Co. 1954.

Tolman, E. C. Collected Papers in Psychology. Berkeley, Cal.: University of California Press. 1951.

Updegraff, Robert R. "The Conscious Use of the Subconscious Mind," Reader's Digest, March 1960.

Van Ormer, Edward B. "Retention After Intervals of Sleep and of Waking." Archives of Psychology, No. 137. New York, May, 1932.

Wagner, A. E. "An Experiment to Determine the Number of Repetitions Necessary to Memorize and Retain with Maximum Certainty a Miscellaneous Collection of Facts." May 1910.

Watson, J. B. The Ways of Behaviorism. New York: Harper & Bros. 1928.

Weinland, James D. How to Improve Your Memory. New York: Barnes & Noble. 1957.